God Wants His Kingdom Back!

Exploring the Lost Purpose of the Church

KDP ISBN: 9798532189706

Contents

Preface

The Rising of the Bride

"I hear the Word has come: 'tis in the Book
That some purport to read and comprehend –
But I do not.

          What need have I to look
And learn such mysteries which but pretend
To light' the burden bound about the head
In lies which blind? No need at all!

                    I see
My purpose well, and have now myriads led
Away from dangerous thought, where Charity
And Justice might conspire to lead astray
Some fools with bright ideas which, tested
On the anvil of reality, lay
Cool and dull now, all their spark arrested.

Bride of the Word, I hide you in my veil:
My word commands the streets – 'Hail, Darkness, hail!'"

This Desecrant enlightenment maligns:
He craves the shadows, loves the stifling air
Which suffocates and tempers Grand Designs
That speak creation's rescue and repair.

Whence came he so, and will he yet prevail?

'Twas loosed in Eden, Garden of Delight,
Long ages past, and soon was heard the wail
Of heavenly agonies. But forthright
Rode the Word, a fleshly Bride to fashion
As a Warrior Queen. But she would not.
Her energies she squanders, and her passion,
And so this glorious quest is left to rot.

Her vision swallowed in the darkened tide,
The Word still 'waits the rising of His Bride…

E. N. R.

Chapter 1

What Are You Doing?

What are you doing?

Take a moment, and let me ask you again...

What on Earth are you doing?

My guess is that you want to give an answer that reflects your values, calling and eternal destiny and that pleases God...that you want to give a comprehensive answer: big questions demand big answers.

What on Earth are you doing?

Such a question invites us to lift our eyes to a greater scheme of existence, challenging our personal desires and self-indulgences.

What of the church of which we are a part, how does she answer this question? With great sadness, I am concerned that much of the Western Church, together with some other sectors of Christendom, currently lacks understanding of God's greater purposes and plans. He has a grand design in which we should all, even now, be engaged. And yet, the church at times seems wholly unconcerned with addressing the question: what on Earth are you doing? Such a display of ignorance and disinterest is a tragedy requiring urgent remedy. According to the Authorised Version (AV), Proverbs 29:18 reads, "where there is no vision, the people perish". A church that has failed to seek and grasp the heaven-given vision for her purpose on Earth is a deep and tragic loss for our world.

Despite best intentions, too often churches have found it more convenient and comfortable to continue with their well-honed programmes and preserve the status quo. This enables the church to stay busy whilst avoiding the deep, foundational work required for necessary change. Questions such as, "Why do we do this?" or, "Why do we do it this way?", if they are even asked, can too frequently be met with the answer: "it's the way it's always been done here". "The way it's always been done here" can become the established pattern for everything from the style of service, the worship music and church seating arrangements to the patterns for mid-week meetings, fundraising activities or the clothes required for participating in a service. It does not take long for a pattern of behaviour to become a habit and then a tradition, because there is comfort and security in perpetuating what has been done before. Perhaps we hear echoes of Jesus' words: "and no one after drinking the old wine wants the new, for he says, 'The old is better'" (Luke 5:39). This "old" wine is well matured, comfortable, familiar and much easier to drink than the "new" by comparison. The more we get used to the "old" wine of past practice, then the harder it becomes to change "the way it's been done around here". However, Jesus shows himself to be no lover of religious tradition! His scathing words to the Pharisees ably demonstrates this:

> "Jesus replied, "And why do you break the command of God for the sake of your tradition?... Thus you nullify the word of God for the sake of your tradition" (Matthew 15:3 & 6).

In order to enjoy God's forthcoming "new" of the future[1], we need to embrace His change in the present.

The launch of the complete Bible translation, known as "Today's English Version" (TEV), in 1976 broke new ground. Not only did it include ingeniously crafted line drawings in the Scriptures – almost like cartoons – but it also carried the tag line that this was "Good News for Modern Man". It was a breath of fresh air to a British church still largely displaying her Victorian form. What's more, over the last 45 years there has been a steady perpetuation of contemporary versions of the Bible from The Passion translation to The Street Bible and The Message, each seeking to bring the living and active word of God to a new generation. These have, indeed, been encouraging developments.

Nevertheless, today's cutting edge is tomorrow's anachronism. Whilst our Christian truths and values are timeless, our presentation of them must have relevance to be

---

[1] "He who was seated on the throne said, 'I am making everything new!'" (Revelation 21:5).

credible. This extends to the ways in which we interact with our communities, be this at local or national levels. It can be argued that great strides are happening in various parts of the church establishment dealing with issues such as the role of women in leadership, the release of the laity into ministry, and purging the clergy ranks of a seeming past immunity to exposure in matters of corruption and immorality. In all honesty, these are not matters for congratulation, but little more than good housekeeping, which should have received careful attention in ages past.

Where is the proactive "Body of Jesus" intent on doing the "Father's business"? Where is the demonstrative embodiment of the Creative Genius who specializes in doing a new thing?

> "Forget the former things; do not dwell on the past. See, I am doing a new thing! Now it springs up; do you not perceive it? I am making a way in the desert and streams in the wasteland" (Isaiah 43:18-19).

Meanwhile, the world continues to move at a great pace. In only the last few decades we have seen: the rise of the cult of celebrity; the dominance of multinational business in setting the agenda of governments; the disintegration of "the family" and rise of post-modernism in Western cultures; the march of Islamic fundamentalism and the ascendancy of environmental awareness. Each of these present-generation trends seems ever to catch the church on the back foot – more likely to react than respond, struggling to know what to say and increasingly tempted to dig deeper into tradition and "how we've always done things" as a defence against the ravages of relentless "progress". So, the church stagnates and misses Heaven's "new thing", for fear of the world's "new thing". How, indeed, do we break out of these patterns of stagnation? And what of God's perspective on what we should be doing?

Throughout history, God has demonstrated a continual longing to communicate, interact and collaborate with people: this is something which naturally flows out of His character. It is also central to His plans and purposes: communication, interaction and collaboration with His people is His plan A for the world. We see evidence for this collaborative methodology throughout history, and indeed throughout our Biblical accounts, where miracles happen as men and women partner with God in releasing the supernatural. In many of these stories there is an "active" element required of the person(s) involved, (in order, some argue, to demonstrate the presence of faith), prior to God's miraculous intervention. A few examples include Moses raising his staff over the Red Sea (Exodus 14:16) and his striking the rock (Exodus 17:6); Elisha having jars collected for oil (2 Kings 4:3), and, from the New Testament, Jesus requiring large jars to be filled first with water before it miraculously becomes wine (John 2:7). God's partnership with humanity in this way is a demonstrable measure of His infinite grace and humility, that He actually chooses us to be His co-workers in fulfilling His purposes.

11

I recall hearing God telling me to invite a particular friend to accompany me in visiting a Masai settlement in Northern Tanzania in 2008. This was quite a random idea as he had never before been to Africa nor shown any special interest there; nevertheless, he came. The result has been an ongoing partnership between the Masai families in question and several church fellowships, which has transformed the lives of the community in Tanzania and become a source of real blessing to the church congregations concerned.

All of this naturally has to start with God's people *knowing* Him and hearing from Him. How this happens is not the subject of this book, suffice to say, all is dependent upon knowing Jesus and enjoying relationship with Him. Indeed, knowing Jesus remains the doorway through which we must pass and the road upon which we must remain if we are to become part of the Church - the People of God.

It may be appropriate here to note that where the word "Church" is printed, with the inclusion of a capital letter, I am referring to the idea of the *ekklesia*[2]. This is the Greek

---

[2] The New Testament Greek word *ekklesia*, having the Old Testament Hebrew counterpart *qahal*, refers to a gathering or assembly of people. This word *qahal* appears some 120 times in the Scriptures of Jesus' day and is consistently translated "assembly", or similar. However, the substitution of the word "church" for *ekklesia* in our current New Testament texts is both puzzling and, some would aver, misleading. This stems from the original meaning behind this *ekkelsia* ("gathering") word not finding full expression in our "church". It was not used to describe just any gathering of people, but those with a particular responsibility for leadership or governance – such as the gathering of a town council. If we embrace this deeper meaning, then the inference is

word translated 'church', as found in Matthew 16:18 when Jesus declares: I will build my e*kklesia*. First and foremost, "*ekklesia*" refers to the redeemed body of believers who enjoy a living, personal relationship with their Lord Jesus, who know themselves to be children of their Father God, and within whom Holy Spirit is residing.

In John 10:9, Jesus says, "I am the gate; whoever enters through me will be saved...", and a little further on "...I know my sheep and my sheep know me" (John 10:14). "Knowing" Jesus is very distinct from "knowing about" Him. This is clear from the original Greek text which points to enjoying a living relationship with Him rather than having a head knowledge about Him[3]. The somewhat reduced brutal logic of His words is clear: if we don't *know* Jesus, then we are not one of the sheep. Of course, this means that we can 'go to' church and not be part of the *ekklesia*. Knowing Jesus is also the means by which we know Father God. Jesus himself said, "I and the Father are one" (John 10:30) and "anyone who has seen me has seen the Father" (John 14:9). Thus, to hear Jesus is to hear the heart of the

---

that Jesus' *ekklesia* of Matthew 16:18 is to be significantly more than mere "pew fodder"; passive, polite and peace-loving acolytes awaiting His rescue mission of a return. Instead, these who know Jesus are to be active participants in the shaping and running of society to His template. This is very different to the popular notion of "church" referring to a building, an institution or even a group of people given to joining together for religious practice. Rather, *ekklesi*a is a movement – of movers, shakers and shapers!

[3] I was surprised to discover this difference myself in the circumstances described later in Chapter 12.

Father, for the Son reveals the Father and does what He sees Him doing[4].

What then do we learn from Jesus of what we should be doing on Earth?

As we progress through this book, we will examine afresh God's answer to the question "What should we be doing?" as well as considering His requirements and resources for the successful completion of His purposes. We will then go on to more fully understand the importance of building His kingdom as we make a rapid sweep through time in Chapters 4 – 7, explaining "God's Grand Design".

What the Western church is actually doing as the Body of Christ, and what we are actually achieving on the wider sphere of planet Earth is not terribly effective outside of our church circles. We touch upon this in Chapters 8 and 9. Too often, Western churches can become insular in their thinking - too often preoccupied with survival in societies where church attendance is plummeting and considered to be an irrelevance. Alternatively, church leaders in other settings may seek to insulate their congregations from harmful worldly temptations in cultures where the power of "sin, the world and the devil" has been wrongly overemphasised. In all such cases, we find churches embattled with a defensive mentality. Regrettably, many appear to be signing up to a new denomination called "The Church of Small Thinking"!

---

[4] (John 17:6 & John 5:19)

Truly, this has to change, and so beginning in Chapter 10 a way forward is proposed. This becomes increasingly practical in the ensuing chapters as we run towards our "Conclusion".

Finally, to imagine God to be smiling benignly upon His broken, hurting creation with something like passive disinterest would be erroneous in the extreme. It would also be an enormous insult to our Creator's loving heart. Through our complicity, the creatures of evil have overrun planet Earth to the point where humanity has become both prey and perpetrators of iniquity. Instead, our God is the most wonderful, loving, caring, compassionate, creative, forgiving Father for whom anyone could ever wish. His mercy is infinite, and His patience with us beyond our understanding. This is the Devoted One whom we see in Jesus not only advocating that we should "go the extra mile" (Matthew 5:41), but more than demonstrating this through His Calvary sacrifice. Words cannot fully describe such an extravagance of love nor depth of self-sacrifice! This is our God who is entirely committed to His creation: and God wants His kingdom back! He wants to revisit our world, not only with His salvation that redeems our eternal destiny – but with a salvation for the whole of society, with His kingdom coming on earth and into all spheres of life with demonstrations of His righteousness and justice. There is a divine exchange available: abundance for lack (2 Corinthians 9:8); gladness instead of mourning (Isaiah 61:3); rejection into community (Psalm 68:6); heartbreak into celebration (Isaiah 62:4) and sickness into a distant memory (Isaiah 58:8)! To Him, this is not an aspiration: it is an achievable reality. Make no mistake, He will see this done!

Let's examine together the critical role that *you* are called to play in this magnificent invasion of Earth's dominion of darkness by heaven's agents of change.

Questions for further consideration:

a) What does it mean for you to *know* Jesus? And what does it mean for God to communicate with you personally?
b) What are you investing into right now that will have eternal consequences?
c) What new or innovative Christian work have you or your local church begun in the last five years?
d) Over what social or international issue do you feel sufficiently strongly to protest or petition "the authorities"?

Chapter 2

Bear Fruit

God wants us to bear fruit. Of all the things that we could be doing, it is this which is His requirement of us.

> "You did not choose me, but I chose you and appointed you to go and bear fruit – fruit that will last" (John 15:16).

Jesus is quite big on fruit! There are accounts of Jesus teaching about the importance of bearing fruit in all four gospels[5]. His emphasis on fruit-bearing and the consequences of not are highlighted when He speaks judgement upon a barren fig tree:

> "Early in the morning, as he was on his way back to the city, he was hungry. Seeing a fig tree by the road, he went up to it but found nothing on it except leaves. Then he said to it, 'May you never bear fruit again!' Immediately the tree withered." (Matthew 21:18-19).

When read alongside Jesus' words in John 15:2 - "He cuts off every branch in me that bears no fruit…" - we begin to

---

[5] See also Matthew 7:17-23; Mark 12:1-9; Luke 6:43 and Luke 13:6-9

grasp the seriousness of our situation. Notice, these unfruitful branches are not growing on some alien vine: these branches are "in Christ" – part of the family!

So, accepting the necessity to "bear fruit" is one thing. However, the question arises, "What fruit?"

It is clear from Matthew 7:15-20 that there are two kinds of fruit. Perhaps predictably termed "good fruit" and "bad fruit", it is important to understand the difference between these two. Good fruit can be thought of as being the "good works" described by Paul:

> "For we are God's workmanship, created in Christ to do good works, which God prepared in advance for us to do" (Ephesians 2:10).

These good works are the resultant outflow of a life fully surrendered to God, and lived in union with Jesus through the indwelling presence of the Spirit of Jesus[6], as He makes clear:

> "Remain in me and I will remain in you. No branch can bear fruit by itself; it must remain in the vine. Neither can you bear fruit unless you remain in me. I am the vine; you are the branches. If a man remains in me and I in him, he will bear much fruit; apart from me you can do nothing. If anyone does

---

[6] Note the terminology of Acts 16:7 in which Holy Spirit is referred to as the "Spirit of Jesus".

not remain in me, he is like a branch that is thrown away and withers; such branches are picked up, thrown into the fire and burned" (John 15:4-6).

Thus, from the indwelling presence of God, we enjoy insight through the mind of God[7] into the purposes of God, so that we may produce good fruit for God by implementing the ideas of God. This is nothing less than the ministry model of Jesus, which is readily available to those who know Him. Conversely, for those who are not operating in union with the Spirit of Jesus – who do not actually 'know' Him – even 'greater' works, such as prophesying, driving out demons and performing many miracles (Matthew 7:22) receive no accolade from Jesus. They only receive the awful condemnation: "away from me you evildoers…" because "I never knew you" (Matthew 7:23). Knowing Jesus - having relationship with Him, being in Him and He in us as our initiator, director and counsellor throughout - is paramount. Any other source for bearing fruit is an imposter, any other manifestation of unnatural power is counterfeit, and any other ministry is false.

Now, it must be conceded that this seems harsh given the majority of kindly individuals' good intentions. Acts of kindness do have intrinsic value, but in the temporal sphere only, and they are not the works nor the fruit of Jesus. To

---

[7] (1 Corinthians 2:16)

.

obtain a more complete picture of this matter it is helpful to introduce two more portions of Scripture:

> "By the grace God has given me, I laid a foundation as an expert builder, and someone else is building on it. But each one should be careful how he builds. For no-one can lay any foundation other than the one already laid, which is Jesus Christ. If any man builds on this foundation using gold, silver, costly stones, wood, hay or straw, his work will be shown for what it is, because the Day will bring it to light. It will be revealed with fire, and the fire will test the quality of each man's work. If what he has built survives, he will receive his reward. If it is burned up, he will suffer loss; he himself will be saved, but only as one escaping through the flames" (1 Corinthians 3:10-15).

> "For we must all appear before the judgement seat of Christ, that each one may receive what is due to him for things done while in the body, whether good or bad" (2 Corinthians 5:10).

Here we have a heavenly revelation of the Judgement Seat of Christ, before which all believers must appear: the purpose being that our works may be judged – things done whilst in the flesh on planet Earth. The proposed mechanism of testing what we have done - or as "builders" what we have been building in the context of ministry - is trial by fire. Some of these "works" survive the testing. Built upon the foundation stone of Jesus, these are the activities, projects and work of those who know Him and set themselves under His authority. On the other hand, some are burned up and perish. This, then, is peculiarly addressed to believers, and so there is some comfort that those whose work is consumed will have their salvation safeguarded. However, it remains troubling that they will proceed, "...only as one escaping through the flames", (1 Corinthians 3:15). I do not want to be one whose works do not make it through the flames. As far as I am able, I want to focus my efforts into durable works which will withstand testing before Jesus. I do not want to ultimately appear before our Father empty-handed and smelling of smoke.

In order, then, to bear good fruit which will last, our ministry activities must satisfy two conditions. The first is that we should be remaining "in the vine"[8] - be in union with Jesus through His indwelling Spirit within each of us. This has to do with who we are, and, most certainly, who we know rather than anything we have actually done. The second condition is shown in the aforementioned Bible passages, albeit less plainly: durable works are those which come from God's ideas rather than from our own good ideas. If we accept that we are "God's workmanship, created to do good works...", then we have equally to accept that these works emanate from God's mind, and are objects of His initiative, since these are things "...which God prepared in advance for

---

[8] John 15: 4

us to do" (Ephesians 2:10). Looking back, I can certainly see times when my ideas predominated over anything God may have wanted to do, sometimes with bizarre effect.

One such incident took place in a very dark, cold and wet inner-city Glasgow street some years ago. I'd been trying to do a little street evangelism without any success. Soaked by the rain, cold and dispirited, I had just had enough and wanted home. Turning to go, I noticed two people with a very large umbrella waving to me to share their shelter as we were going in the same direction. However, due to the darkness I couldn't distinguish who they were until I ducked underneath their brolly. I was a bit surprised to find them to be a Chinese couple with plainly no English language between them. With renewed hope and faith rising within me I reckoned that these were the reason I'd been pacing Glasgow's streets. I was now about to enjoy the provision of a "divine appointment". My only impediment was language…

It was then that I had a bright idea. Grasping the nettle, I began softly speaking in tongues, and growing in confidence tried to make them sound as "Chinese" as possible. I was hoping that God could make such sense of my babble that they'd hear the gospel in this way, understand it and respond. I actually had a precedent for this uppermost in my mind as a friend had just so received Spanish in a not too dissimilar fashion, and I thought I might well try and do the same! Those poor people who had generously welcomed me out of the rain – what must they have thought as I whined, intoned and "pinged" my way through a repertoire of gibberish? They were absolute courtesy itself, but probably never again invited a stranger under their umbrella for fear of further lunacy. I have to admit, it was not a great idea.

Thankfully, God's ways and thoughts are different from ours, and Peter tells Jesus that only He has the words of eternal life, and no-one else (John 6:68). Could not the same be true regarding works of eternal standing, durability or significance? Only the plans or projects that originate from the mind of Christ, and which are implemented in obedience to His direction, are the ministry activities which will endure the testing of fire and be recognised by rewards to ourselves.

Our bearing good fruit which lasts is dependent on "being" in relationship with God and "doing" in obedience to God's leading and command. In terms of our earlier building site analogy, knowing the architect is key[9], for out of this we receive our instructions about what to build next: Jesus is the one with the completed design in his head and the knowledge of how to achieve it.

However, whilst working successfully on a physical building site might be a matter of following instructions and staying out of trouble, this falls very short of God's ways. God has never intended that we relate to Him as workers, employees, servants or slaves. Rather, He calls us "friends" (John 15:15). Jesus has made known to His friends

---

[9] Hebrews 11:10

everything that He has learned from the Father, and this leads us to a further prerequisite for durable fruit bearing ministry: *understanding*, which we will explore next.

Questions for further consideration:

a) How can we be certain that we are "remaining in the vine"?
b) What past activity can you recognise with certainty as one of God's ideas?
c) What past activity do you suspect was very much one of your own ideas?
d) Can you say you know yourself to be a "friend" of God?
e) What future purpose or calling do you know to be God's idea?

Chapter 3

Understanding

If Jesus is big on fruit, He is also big on understanding!

This is well illustrated through Jesus' telling of the parable of the sower - a parable that is not, as it has often been presented, primarily an instruction on evangelism strategy, but instead a teaching about the importance of understanding.

> "When anyone hears the message about the kingdom and does not *understand* it, the evil one comes and snatches away what was sown in his heart. This is the seed sown along the path…but the one who received the seed that fell on good soil is the man who hears the word and *understands* it. He produces a crop, yielding a hundred, sixty or thirty times what was sown" (Matthew 13:19 & 23).

The seed falls on different soil, and the key ingredient in the soil which produces the crop - or "fruitfulness" - is *understanding*. This is also the missing element, to a greater or lesser degree, with each of the places in which the seed does not take root long enough to bear fruit: those who failed to receive the seed lacked complete understanding. There are numerous enemy strategies to achieve this end: distraction, derision, deception, one might even include delusion here.

I once shared the gospel with a lady only to be told very firmly by her that she didn't need Jesus. When I asked why, she very matter-of-factly replied that she was perfect! For me, the sad truth was that she really believed this, as became evident from our subsequent conversation.

Jesus describes in the parable how the seed falls on shallow, stony soil so that only a meagre root forms: these people have received the message with minimal understanding. Many receive a simple theology which tells them that "everything will be easy and well if you receive this message from God". This sort of understanding cannot endure the challenges of external pressures, persecutions or disappointments, so this superficial seedling dies.

I remember a gifted young Kenyan man setting out to follow a call into missions. However, in the face of opposition from his family members, he quickly renounced this future for himself. Similarly, a young woman, directed by God to college, dropped out of her studies upon finding difficulty in making friends. Why? Because she knew "Jesus would not want me to be unhappy".

Such a statement does not sit well with so many of Jesus' warnings and teachings about the expectations that we should have as His followers. He warns, "you will be handed over to be persecuted and put to death, and you will be hated by all the nations because of me" (Matthew 23:9). Jesus never preached an easy gospel. In fact, rather than promising a life devoid of challenges, He did the opposite, talking candidly about the cost:

> "If anyone would come after me, he must deny himself and take up his cross and follow me" (Mark 8:34)[10].

This leads me to suggest that there is such a thing as "bad evangelism" – or perhaps the more familiar expression "cheap grace", as coined by Dietrich Bonhoeffer in his book "The cost of Discipleship". This is actually contributing to a delay in building God's kingdom rather than hastening it. It presents an inadequate, "soft" gospel, which promises "life will be easy, and all will be well if you come to Jesus". Another version says, "Jesus doesn't want anyone to go to hell, so don't worry, do what you like – just remember to say 'Sorry' afterwards"! These are all lies and deception. They promise a broad easy path, when Jesus warned it would be narrow; they promise an easy life, when Paul clearly states we are "living sacrifices". "Soft gospel" promises produce Christians who are either unready or unwilling to "take up [their] cross daily" (Luke 9:23 – my parentheses) and follow Jesus. Consequently, a watching world notes people who preach one set of values, but who fail to live them out in their own behaviour. And as such, the reputation of Jesus suffers

---

[10] See also: Mark 8:34-38; Mark 13:9-13; Luke 9:57-62; Luke 14:25-33; John 15:18-20.

and His kingdom cause is discredited by the charges of hypocrisy levelled against His perceived followers.

Jesus goes on to describe a soil that is basically good - adequate for increased growth and development, with better root depth - although the seed falls "among the thorns". This time the attack arrives from within. The distraction of worries and the deception of wealth - fear and finances - are particular satanic strategies which he uses to undermine the faith and confidence which believers are to find in God alone. Jesus describes here people who have a genuine saving trust in God which can weather life's externally imposed storms. However, they lack an understanding of the demonic strategies that oppose us and the authority which we have, as God's people, to triumph over these devices. Too easily "sheep" fall prey to the "roaring lion" (1 Peter 5:8) through ignorance or through denying that such a creature exists.

I remember a particularly industrious and tireless Christian lady who gave herself valiantly to church activities and business. Despite this enthusiasm, she flatly refuted any idea of the devil. Instead, evil was an abstract influence – a dark force loosed among the children of Adam.

However, Jesus is clear in the parable that seed that falls on essentially good soil, is still often subject to "thorns". These seeds do not die but remain "unfruitful" or "immature" (Luke 8:14), which equally indicates an inability to bear fruit. This describes so much activity of valiant brothers and sisters - maybe even your own situation - pressing on with church activities, whilst labouring under intense personal behavioural or mental difficulties, and subsequent feelings of deep private guilt or financial distractions. It is all too common for our own brothers and sisters to be agonising under every kind of oppression, from one assault after another, unaware of their vulnerability - the ongoing battles, without respite, rendering them ultimately fruitless.

Finally, Jesus describes those who receive the seed and produce harvests of varying amounts as those who have received the seed "with understanding" (verse 23); (perhaps the differing yields even indicate greater or lesser measures of understanding). It is worth noticing that such understanding – and the subsequent great fruitfulness - was within the grasp of a group of first century "unschooled" fishermen:

> "When they saw the courage of Peter and John and realised that they were unschooled, ordinary men, they were astonished, and they took note that these men had been with Jesus" (Acts of the Apostles 4:13).

Thus, it is something for which we all may reach with expectation by God's grace. Whatever our educational background, IQ or natural ability, there is ample encouragement from the mouth of Jesus to run with confidence after understanding. He can and will make clear all that He longs to reveal to us.

Jesus does indeed long for His disciples to have increasing understanding, in order that they may bear much fruit, just as Paul also prayed: "we have not stopped praying for you and asking God to fill you with the knowledge of his will through all spiritual wisdom and understanding" (Colossians 1:9). This is not a head-based understanding, but a spiritual one.

By way of illustration, we can turn to the account concerning Mary and Martha in the gospels, where, in Luke 10:38-42, Jesus is a guest at the home of the sisters. It's a familiar story: Martha is busying herself to the point of distraction with all of the practical work, having shopped and cleaned, she is now cooking and hosting the entire party of those travelling with Jesus, providing water for their washing and ensuring they feel welcome and comfortable. Meanwhile, Mary appears oblivious to all of this and is sitting at the feet of Jesus. She is fixed upon His face and hanging upon His every word so as to be totally lost in Him, drinking deeply of His presence. Martha asks Jesus to rebuke Mary and instead He comes to Mary's defence: Mary has "chosen better" by her actions. Now skip forward to John 12:1-8, Jesus is again with Mary and Martha, but now also their brother Lazarus is with them. In a remarkable act of generosity Mary pours a most expensive perfume over Jesus' feet, much to the chagrin of Judas who begrudges a "year's wages" being squandered in such a way. Who comes to Mary's defence this time? Again, it is Jesus, but what is more remarkable however, is that Jesus explains that in so doing, Mary has anointed Him for burial. What an extraordinary thing to say! This is the Messiah speaking: God incarnate! Who on Earth in their wildest nightmare could imagine the impossible – that God was going to die – and what's more (as it turns out), in just a week's time? We find Mary here having done exactly the most appropriate thing at exactly the right time. How did she understand to do this and to do it now? It is this spiritual understanding which she demonstrates, coming not from exhaustive theological study, (valuable as this may be), but from spending time with Jesus, just as she had done in Luke 10. It is worth emphasising here that time spent with Jesus is never time wasted: it changes us! And what of Martha now, during this last week with Jesus? Well, Martha served (John 12:2).

So then, what is it that we are to understand? This is key to releasing the fruitfulness we are to seek. The answer to this is not in the soil, but rather in the seed. For the seed we are to understand is the message of the kingdom of God (verse 19). Too often, this message is confused with the message of the gospel of salvation. It is my contention that this gospel of the kingdom is a much bigger gospel than the salvation message often preached so heartily from pulpits these near two millennia past. If the gospel of salvation speaks of God's love and longing for mankind, then the gospel of the kingdom shouts of God's Grand Design!

Questions for further consideration:

a) What type of soil do you most closely identify with today from the parable of the sower?
b) Can you think of an externally imposed challenge to your Christian faith which you have successfully overcome?
c) Can you think of a time when you battled worry or financial pressure that may have been part of a spiritual battle in your life?
d) Where are you producing the most fruit right now?

Chapter 4

God's Grand Design: Construction

As with all construction jobs, it's best to start at foundation level and work upwards. With this in mind, we begin at the very start.

Genesis 1 opens with, "In the beginning God created…", leaving us in no doubt that God is the source and protagonist of our universe. However, the English translation fails to capture a significant detail of the original Hebrew text: "God" in this very first verse in the scriptures is the Hebrew word "*Elohim*", which is plural. It would perhaps be more accurately rendered "Gods". Clearly, translators faced a choice here at their very outset: communicate the truthful essence of who is responsible for creation or open up a polytheistic confusion. They have consistently and wisely chosen the former. Even so, there are some important insights to be gained from this hidden plurality, namely that this is the first appearance of the idea that God is actually "Trinity". This idea is introduced right at the very beginning of God's revelation of Himself. The concept of the Trinity is a great mystery; the Bible does not address it explicitly, but throughout the scriptures we find glimpses of the triune nature of our One God. These Trinity "pointers" are scattered throughout the scriptures. God refers to Himself in the plural at various points, particularly in the early chapters of Genesis[11], whilst right at the start of Jesus' ministry we see the three members of the Trinity line up vertically from earth to heaven:

> "As Jesus was coming up out of the water, he saw heaven being torn open and the Spirit descending on him like a dove. And a voice came from heaven; 'You are my Son, whom I love; with you I am well pleased'" (Mark 1:10-11).

The means by which the members of the Trinity cooperate and practically function is outside the scope of this publication. However, it is significant to notice that each Trinity member was active in the creation process.

> "…yet for us there is but one God, the Father, from whom all things came and for whom we live; and there is but one Lord, Jesus Christ, through whom all things came and through whom we live" (1 Corinthians 8:6).

It is from the Father that "all things came"; this includes the entire creation, as the Bible makes clear from Genesis 1 onwards[12]. Creation flows out from the Father; but what of Jesus?

---

[11] Genesis 1:26; Genesis 11:7
[12] Psalm 33 vs 6-9; Psalm 102:25; John 1; Hebrew 11:3.

Continuing to read 1 Corinthians 8:6 reveals that whilst all things came from the Father, in some way they also came "through" Jesus. Similarly, John tells us in his opening prose:

> "Through him [Jesus] all things were made; without him nothing was made that has been made" (John 1:3).

Paul reiterates this in his letter to the Hebrews:

> "…but in these last days he has spoken to us by his Son, whom he appointed heir of all things, and through whom he made the universe" (Hebrews 1:2).

In fact, Jesus' centrality to the creative process is emphasised:

> "For by him all things were created: things in heaven and on earth, visible and invisible, whether thrones or powers or rulers or authorities; all things were created by him and for him" (Colossians 1:16).

There is no doubt that Jesus was involved in the work of creation. The diagram in Figure 1 illustrates how we might think about creation flowing out from the Father and the outpouring passing "through" Jesus.

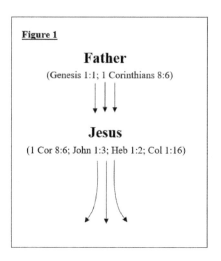

Figure 1

Father

(Genesis 1:1; 1 Corinthians 8:6)

Jesus

(1 Cor 8:6; John 1:3; Heb 1:2; Col 1:16)

Genesis 1:2 now presents an apparently chaotic picture, translated in varying ways into English. The NIV translates it:

> "Now the earth was formless and empty, darkness was over the surface of the deep, and the Spirit of God was hovering over the waters" (Genesis 1:2).

This disorder is contrary to the nature of God, who is a God of order[13], and there is much for Him to do before His work is completed. Above this formless void, we find Holy Spirit, fully engaged in creation, moving over and overshadowing what is and what is yet to be.

---

[13] 1 Corinthians 14:33

So, our diagram can be further updated (Figure 2), with the end result: paradise (Genesis 1:31). God looks at this declaring it is not just "good", but "very good"!

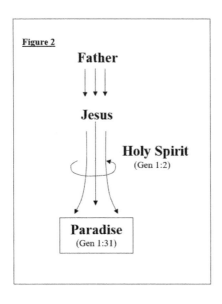

With the construction phase completed, authority for the ongoing welfare and maintenance of this created world is plainly delegated to mankind: God gives humanity a "Dominion Mandate" - a commission to establish control and governmental sovereignty.

> "And God blessed them, and God said unto them,
> 'Be fruitful and multiply, and replenish the earth,

and subdue it: and have dominion over the fish of the sea, and the fowl of the air, and over every living thing that moveth upon the earth" (Genesis 1:28 AV).

This is further echoed in the psalms:

"You made him [humanity] ruler over all the works of your hands; you put everything under his feet, all flocks and herds, and the beasts of the field, the birds of the air, and the fish of the sea, all that swim the paths of the seas" (Psalm 8:6-8).

So far, so (very) good, however, catastrophe is not far away...

Chapter 5

God's Grand Design: Collapse

One of God's greatest, and perhaps most dangerous, gifts to humanity is our free will: the capacity to disagree with God to the point of rebellion. This was also bestowed on the angelic host. In their case, a significant proportion of them chose to follow an exalted angel (Lucifer) who wished to set himself up in the place of God. This was a direct challenge to God's sovereignty. Isaiah's prophecies tell some of Satan's story:

> "How you have fallen from heaven, O morning star, son of the dawn! You have been cast down to the earth, you who once laid low the nations! You said in your heart, 'I will ascend to heaven; I will raise my throne above the stars of God; I will sit enthroned on the mount of assembly, on the utmost heights of the sacred mountain. I will ascend above the tops of the clouds; I will make myself like the Most High'. But you are brought down to the grave, to the depths of the pit" (Isaiah 14:12-15).

Ezekiel similarly describes Satan's pride and subsequent expulsion from heaven:

"You were the model of perfection, full of wisdom and perfect in beauty. You were in Eden, the garden of God; every precious stone adorned you: ruby, topaz and emerald, chrysolite, onyx and jasper, sapphire, turquoise and beryl. Your settings and mountings were made of gold; on the day you were created they were prepared. You were anointed as a guardian cherub, for so I ordained you. You were on the holy mount of God; you walked among the fiery stones. You were blameless in your ways from the day you were created till wickedness was found in you. Through your widespread trade you were filled with violence, and you sinned. So I drove you in disgrace from the mount of God, and I expelled you, O guardian cherub, from among the fiery stones. Your heart became proud on account of your splendour. So I threw you to the earth; I made a spectacle of you before kings" (Ezekiel 28:12-17).

The consequence of this rebellion was "war in heaven" (Revelation 12:7) during which the warrior archangel Michael and his loyal host defeated the usurper, identified as Satan in Revelation 12:9. His fate was to be "hurled to the earth", which is corroborated in Ezekiel 28:17, and was witnessed by Jesus:

> "He replied, 'I saw Satan fall as lightening from heaven'" (Luke 10:18).

The stage is set: Satan is now on planet Earth and has access to Adam and Eve in Eden.

Unsurprisingly, Satan's original and only strategy soon emerges - to take the place of God. We see this in Isaiah 14:13-14, in his invitation for Jesus to worship him (Luke 4:7), and in the emergence of this theme during his temptation of Eve. Whilst the physical attributes of sight and sustenance by the forbidden fruit were apparently alluring to her, they played no part in Satan's appeal to transgress. Instead, his whole argument to Eve may be summarised by an extract from Genesis 3:4: "...and you will be like God..." This was the prize that he personally found to be so irresistible, the most convincing carrot, in his estimation, which could be dangled in front of any creature, and it does much to reveal his heart's desire and ambition.

So, in Eden's garden we find Satan conniving to take the place of God through his relationship with mankind and win dominance over the earth at least, if not in heaven. He seeks to exploit the precious gift of freewill given to humanity at creation, introducing the choice to listen to him instead of God. Doubt is planted into Eve's mind about the goodness and kindness of God and she is readily persuaded, together with Adam, to go along with the suggestion of eating from the tree of the knowledge of good and evil. Eating its fruit is in direct disobedience to God's command:

"…but you must not eat from the tree of the knowledge of good and evil, for when you eat of it you will surely die" (Genesis 2:17).

The consequences are cataclysmic. Several things happen simultaneously. Humanity sins for the first time; we fall vulnerable to a now ongoing capacity to sin and die, and we erect a barrier between ourselves and God which only Jesus will ultimately demolish. However, beyond this, and of extreme importance, is that a transfer of authority happens during Genesis 3:6. The Dominion Mandate of Genesis 1:28 gave authority over the Earth into humanity's hands. Tragically, this is given away to Satan only two chapters later. Our disobedience to God cancels out our previous submission to Him, and our preferred compliance to Satan's instruction now brings us, and all that we possess, under his domain. This includes our authority, or "dominion" over this world in which we live. This is now surrendered, or submitted, to our new overlord of choice. Thus it is that John can write that, "the whole world is under the control of the evil one" (1 John 5:19). Furthermore, Jesus calls the devil the "prince of this world" (John 12:31; John 14:30; John 16:11), and when Satan boasts of the nations that, "…all their splendour and authority has been given to me…" (Luke 4:6) Jesus does not shout "Liar!". Satan was actually speaking the truth: a truth literally as old as Eden.

It is a simple reality of nature that we seek to put our stamp on or infuse our values throughout the domain in which we have authority. We see this at a human level in our family values, and at a divine level in the kingdom of God: the kingdom of God is nothing less than a tangible manifestation of the character of God. We see it further in the fallen world which Satan has corrupted to his likeness and liking. With this infernal usurper in control of world affairs it is little wonder that the world is such a place of moral darkness and suffering. It is also understandable that "natural disasters" should regularly feature in the present world order. They all bear the stamp of its current ruler. It is therefore lamentable that God wrongly receives the blame for these so-called "acts of God", and that His reputation is dragged lower and lower by accusations that He should "Do something about it!"

So then, what is to be done?

Chapter 6

God's Grand Design: Completion

God wants this world's kingdom back!

The gospels shout this through the parables and pronouncements of Jesus: this is His number one priority.

When Jesus provides His disciples with a model for prayer, His first request after addressing His Father in heaven, His prime thrust, the first item on His prayer list, is that God's kingdom would come on Earth (Matthew 6:10) in exactly the same way as it is in heaven. This is echoed again just a few verses later:

> "But seek first his kingdom and his righteousness, and all these things will be given you as well" (Matthew 6:33).

Jesus' command was not to seek first the salvation of souls, but rather God's kingdom. Jesus taught that:

> "the kingdom of heaven is like treasure hidden in a field. When a man found it, he hid it again, and then in his joy went and sold all he had and bought that field. Again, the kingdom of heaven is like a merchant looking for fine pearls. When he found

one of great value, he went away and sold everything he had and bought it" (Matthew 13:44-45).

Laying a hold of God's kingdom is to be our foremost priority. We even see this in the acclamation long awaited in heaven:

> "The kingdom of the world has become the kingdom of our Lord and of his Christ, and he will reign for ever and ever." (Revelation 11:15).

This will be a cause for great celestial rejoicing, as evidenced in the verses following:

> "And the twenty-four elders, who were seated on their thrones before God, fell on their faces and worshipped God saying, 'We give thanks to you Lord God Almighty, the One who is and who was, because you have taken your great power and have begun to reign. The nations were angry; and your wrath has come. The time has come for judging the dead, and for rewarding your servants the prophets and your saints and those who reverence your name, both small and great – and for destroying those who destroy the earth'" (Revelation 11:16-18).

The dominance of this theme does not abate: as Jesus' earthly ministry draws to a close, after His agonising death, descent into the depths (1 Peter 3:19), glorious resurrection and release of Holy Spirit to His disciples (John 20:22), He has a few short weeks to prepare them for the coming trials and persecutions. Imagine the questions occupying the disciples' minds - the wealth of subjects around which their conversation with Jesus would dance and dwell! And yet, we find Jesus returning again to this same theme:

> "...He appeared to them over a period of forty days and spoke about the kingdom of God" (Acts of the Apostles 1:3b).

All because this is His number one priority: God wants His kingdom back!

So, will God do something about it? Make no mistake, He has already done so. He has sacrificed Himself on our behalf to redeem the error of Eden, and to provide for a regime change in the world we know. To go beyond this with apocalyptic intervention at this time would mean Him taking back the gift of freewill and reducing living beings to mere automatons. So, instead, out of His inexhaustible grace, and as an act of selfless love, He has chosen another way. He has provided the means necessary for us to win back what we gave away to the enemies of God and man. It is the People of God who are charged with the task of re-establishing God's righteous rule on planet Earth, those who accept His open invitation to relationship with Him and choose to ally themselves with this cause. In short, *we* are to rebuild His kingdom.

This has been the case from the outset of Jesus' ministry, our ultimate role model. In the gospel accounts we find Jesus not only to be the itinerant preacher and teacher but also the One who readily combats the consequences of Satan's destructive control over people. These consequences include the ravages of sickness and demonic possession, which exercises both control and torment. Wherever the demonic rears its ugly head, Jesus takes a confrontational approach to bring release to those afflicted; he is never apologetic nor conciliatory. There is nothing soft or passive about this Man - "gentle Jesus meek and mild" is a caricature missing from the gospels. Rather, He is the Liberator, the Lover and the Leader! This is entirely consistent with His Messianic Commission from the Father, which He Himself articulated at Nazareth:

> "The Spirit of the Lord is upon me, because He has anointed me to preach good news to the poor. He has sent me to proclaim freedom for the prisoners and recovery of sight for the blind, to release the oppressed, to proclaim the year of the Lord's favour" (Luke 4:18-19),

and then owned in Luke 4:21,

> "…and he began by saying to them, 'Today this scripture is fulfilled in your hearing'".

What's more, He has passed this commission on to those who follow Him, the Church (Mark 1:16-18; Mark 3:13-15). Such a call to follow Jesus is not a call to peace and rest in our external circumstances – though this is at odds with the expectations of many - on the contrary, peace and rest are the internalized riches of the Church.

> "'Peace I leave with you; my peace I give you. I do not give to you as the world gives. Do not let your hearts be troubled and do not be afraid'" (John 14:27).

> "'Come to me all you who are weary and burdened, and I will give you rest. Take my yoke upon you and learn from me, for I am gentle and humble in heart, and you will find rest in your souls. For my yoke and burden is light'" (Matthew 11:28-30).

These gifts of peace and rest are to be enjoyed in the midst of battle (John 16:33)! Amongst all else, the Church is called to be a Warrior People. Why? Because God wants His kingdom back! It is this alone which can ultimately provide the complete solution to the bondage, hopelessness and destruction which typifies the tyrannical control of our current world ruler.

Jesus foresaw this looming cosmic war, and the first recorded occasion in which "Church", (or more accurately, the Greek *ekklesia*), is mentioned in the Bible is in the context of warfare:

> "And I say unto thee, that thou art Peter, and upon
> this rock I will build my church; and the gates of hell
> shall not prevail against it" (Matthew 16:18 AV).

The picture here is of a Church militant and on the offensive. She is not embattled by enemy strategies, retreating or defensive, rather the opposite is promised by Jesus: hell's gates, symbolically guarding the entrance to Satan's stronghold, will not be sturdy enough to withstand the terrifying onslaught of the Church. Jesus' expectations for the Church were clear from both His words and actions: the kingdom was to advance, and this forcefully! Note the timescale and description by which Jesus identifies those who are called to this task:

> "From the days of John the Baptist until now, the
> kingdom of heaven has been forcefully advancing,
> and forceful men lay hold of it" (Matthew 11:12).

Furthermore, the outcome is not in question. Victory over our common enemy is guaranteed, fulfilling God's hidden purpose from ages past, which Paul names as, "...to bring all things in heaven and on earth under one head, even Christ" (Ephesians 1: 9-10). Jesus' rule and reign over all things will one day be universally acknowledged, (as in the whole universe), with every tongue declaring it and every knee bowing (Philippians 2:6-11). The supremacy of Christ has, in fact, always been this way, (rather than expedient in response to the fall), since from the beginning all things were made "for" Jesus, as well as "by" or "through" Him

49

(Colossians 1:16). This bringing of all things together under Christ is the reality and hallmark of the kingdom of God on Earth. God's desire is for our inner selves to be freely submitted to His Lordship, along with every sphere of influence on the earth. The mission of toppling Satan from his place of self-elevation and restoring the kingdom under the righteous headship of Jesus can now be added to our diagrammatic representation in Figure 3.

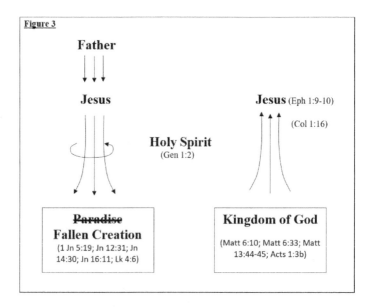

Figure 3

Father

Jesus

Jesus (Eph 1:9-10)

(Col 1:16)

Holy Spirit
(Gen 1:2)

~~Paradise~~
Fallen Creation
(1 Jn 5:19; Jn 12:31; Jn 14:30; Jn 16:11; Lk 4:6)

Kingdom of God
(Matt 6:10; Matt 6:33; Matt 13:44-45; Acts 1:3b)

The question now arises as to how we are expected to defeat what Paul describes as "the powers of this dark world", and "the spiritual forces of evil"? For he rightly asserts that "our struggle is not against flesh and blood" (Ephesians 6:12).

If we are to engage a spiritual enemy in combat, then we need sufficient spiritual help, spiritual authority and spiritual power. Thank God He has satisfied our needs in all these things! Moreover, He has done it with no less than the provision of Himself. The Church is generally considered to have been birthed on the Day of Pentecost, as recorded in Acts of the Apostles 2. Jesus had promised this occasion and cautioned His followers to wait for it (Acts 1:4-8), eager that they should be suitably equipped before being launched into the spiritual battle ahead.

> "On one occasion, while he was eating with them, he gave them this command: 'Do not leave Jerusalem, but wait for the gift my Father promised, which you have heard me speak about. For John baptised with water, but in a few days you will be baptised with the Holy Spirit.'
>
> So when they met together, they asked him, 'Lord, are you at this time going to restore the kingdom to Israel?'
>
> He said to them, 'It is not for you to know the times or dates the Father has set by his own authority. But you will receive power when the Holy Spirit comes on you; and you will be my witnesses in Jerusalem, and in all Judea and Samaria, and to the ends of the earth'" (Acts of the Apostles 1:4-8).

The word "witnesses" in Acts 1:8 in the Greek suggests a commissioning by Jesus to be a "martyr people". As such, we are to understand that the way forward will not be easy, but we will not be advancing alone. In all this, the marvel of Pentecost is that God came in Person to empower His Church, in the form of Holy Spirit, to preside over the imminent campaign. It is He who provides:

> "The weapons we fight with (which) are not the weapons of this world. On the contrary, they have divine power to demolish strongholds." (2 Corinthians 10:4). (My inclusions in parentheses.)

This "empowering" by Holy Spirit is not the universal or continuous experience of Christians everywhere. It has been my own experience to receive two significant visitations from Holy Spirit. Firstly, He came to reside in me when I became a Christian. It was this which secured my position in Christ and in His Body the Church; His indwelling Spirit is His 'seal' – a deposit guaranteeing my inheritance in Christ (Ephesians 1:13-14). Similarly, Jesus breathed on the disciples in John 20:22, saying as He did so: "Receive the Holy Spirit". This was not an accidental consequence of His standing too close whilst exhaling! It was rather something very personal and purposeful. "Breath" and "Spirit" have long been connected in Jewish thinking, as exemplified by the Hebrew word "*ruach*" sharing the double meaning of both "breath" and "spirit". When Jesus prophetically expels His breath over the disciples, He imparts His Spirit to the disciples in one moment. This was no longer the earth-bound man Jesus, but the risen Christ, sharing some of the first fruits of His recent Easter triumph.

Did it work? Did they receive the presence of Holy Spirit, or did they not? It would take a rash man or woman to tell Jesus this attempt didn't work, and He'd have to have another go a few weeks later! Even so, these disciples - who had already received the presence of Holy Spirit - were waiting in Jerusalem on the Day of Pentecost in obedience to Jesus (Luke 24:49). As promised, Holy Spirit visits again, bringing His "baptism" or "fullness" (Acts 1:5; Acts 2:4). This time it was not a primary impartation of His presence, but rather of His power. In my own case, this second "Pentecost" experience came some nine years after receiving Jesus - and only after I had become aware that such was available and was hungering for all that He had for me. It was through this second encounter, this "filling", that I discovered I had the "power from on high" promised by Jesus. Additionally, I now had Holy Spirit's gifts at my disposal (1 Corinthians 12:8-10). This second, or "Pentecost", experience was never intended by God to be a "bonus ball" for the lucky few. Rather it is an essential equipping for all His Church to accomplish all her purposes under God and so win her glorious prize. We need to appropriate this power and step out in our God-given authority to use it in our spiritual callings and combat. Our diagram can now be modified to include this entrance by Holy Spirit moving over, around and through the Church for completing God's "Grand Design", as in Figure 4.

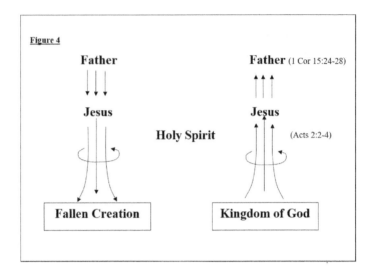

Figure 4

Finally, the exaltation of Jesus over all things is not the ultimate destination of time and space. There is yet one further act to this drama: Father, Son and Holy Spirit function in mutually submitted perfection, and with inclusive honouring and order. This is always characteristic of the workings of the Trinity. So it is then, that when Jesus is elevated over all things He will give the kingdom to God the Father:

> "Then the end will come, when he hands over the kingdom to God the Father after he has destroyed all dominion, authority and power. For He must reign until he has put all his enemies under his feet. The last enemy to be destroyed is death. For he 'has put

everything under his feet'. Now when it says 'everything' has been put under him, it is clear that this does not include God himself, who put everything under Christ. When he has done this, then the Son himself will be made subject to him who put everything under him, so that God may be all in all" (1 Corinthians 15:24-28).

The addition of this to Figure 4 completes a picture enjoying such symmetry and balance as to possess a beauty of its own. It speaks of God's order and strategy, even in the face of enemy interference. It has the appearance of God breathing out creation, and then breathing it back into Himself. Notwithstanding the seeming chaos of the ages, there is an elegant simplicity and poise hidden behind the Almighty's "Grand Design"!

Even so, at this point, there is still something missing…

Chapter 7

God's Grand Design: The Cross

The cross has been described as the turning point of history: the hinge pin of all cosmic order. There is but one place for the cross to sit: right at the centre of God's plan. The cross is God's redemptive masterstroke of self-sacrificial genius - at which all heaven must have stared open-mouthed, and our enemy slavered with jubilant, premature delight, before realising that this was a cruciform victory.

It would be more accurate to refer to the cross and the resurrection as a combined entity, and not the cross alone as the defining breakthrough of God's liberating purposes for His creation. Paul writes that, "I resolved to know nothing while I was with you except Jesus Christ and him crucified" (1 Corinthians 2:2). However, it is plain from his other writings that he placed equal importance and weight on the fact of Jesus' resurrection: to the Philippians church he writes, "I want to know Christ and the power of his resurrection" (3:10).[14] It is in this resurrection that we see the irrefutable evidence of the power of our "last enemy" – death - being destroyed (1 Corinthians 15:26). Indeed, we can now rejoice that Jesus, "having disarmed the powers and

---

[14] See also Romans 6:5 and 1 Corinthians 15:13-19.

authorities… made a public spectacle of them, triumphing over them by the cross" (Colossians 2:15).

Now, the expression "powers and authorities" is worthy of some expansion. The original Greek word from which we receive the English "powers" is "*archas*". Paul uses this term to refer to angels and demons holding dominions entrusted to them, and so in Colossians 2:15 "powers" most certainly identifies demonic rulers rather than human dignitaries. The corresponding Greek word which is translated "authorities" is "*exousias*". This means one upon whom power is conferred or authority, and again here identifies a spiritual or demonic being rather than any human agency. This understanding is reinforced by Paul using the same "*exousias*" word in Ephesians 6:12, where he writes,

> "For our struggle is not against flesh and blood, but against the rulers, against the authorities, against the powers of this dark world and against the spiritual forces of evil in the heavenly realms".

Thus, in Colossians 2:15, is the efficacy of the death and resurrection of Jesus proclaimed by Paul.

Further affirmation can be found in the gospels regarding the successful transfer of authority back to Jesus. As already mentioned, early on in Luke's gospel, Satan is found bragging about the authority he has over all the nations of the world:

> "The devil led him up to a high place and showed him in an instant all the kingdoms of the world. And he said to him, 'I will give you all their authority and splendour, for it is has been given to me, and I can give it to anyone I want to" (Luke 4:5-6).

However, from the other side of the cross, Jesus legitimately declares,

> "All authority in heaven and on earth has been given to me" (Matthew 28:18).

Hallelujah! Job done!

But how can we see and experience the fruit of this authority transfer in our daily lives? It is helpful to first understand the difference between authority and power. Power is the ability to effect change or influence; authority is the legitimacy to exercise power.

A good example of this is a uniformed policeman bearing a gun. His uniform proclaims his authority, and his gun gives him the power to enforce it. When he draws his gun and commands us to stop, we do so because ignoring him may involve being shot. However, our refusal to obey him would additionally bring down upon our heads the whole weight of the prevailing legal system and its consequences. Now imagine this policeman loses his job, forfeits his uniform, but manages to keep his gun. He still has the power to coerce through his gun, but not the legal authority to do this. Thus, when he now draws his gun and commands us to stop – he is still powerful, but he has no legitimate authority: we are no longer legally obliged to obey. In fact, mindful that he is now acting illegally, as a gun-toting radical outside the law, it may be deemed a service to society to engage him in combat, disarm him, and render him powerless. At our present point in history, here stands Satan. He is waving his gun to powerful effect, but has been stripped of his authority. The Church, instead, has had the authority restored so she can engage him in combat and render him powerless.

The cross and the resurrection is the watershed event of the ages through which our struggles with Satan's dominion of darkness, (Colossians 1:13), and bondage to sin and death are broken once and for all through Jesus' Easter victory. For those who will receive Him, the indwelling Spirit of Jesus now brings spiritual life and freedom to our persons,

> "…because through Christ Jesus the law of the Spirit of life has set me free from the law of sin and death" (Romans 8:2).

Indeed, not only this, but we additionally receive a new power and authority over our enemy and his schemes:

> "I pray also that the eyes of your heart may be enlightened in order that you may know the hope to which he has called you, the riches of his glorious inheritance in the saints, and his incomparably great power for us who believe. That power is like the

working of his mighty strength, which he exerted in Christ when he raised him from the dead and seated him at his right hand in the heavenly realms, far above every rule and authority, power and dominion, and every title that can be given, not only in the present age, but also in the one to come" (Ephesians 1:18-21).

A foretaste of this authority was exercised by Jesus' twelve disciples during His earthly ministry (Mark 6:7,13) and later by a larger group to their amazement and joy who reported: "Lord, even the demons submit to us in your name" (Luke 10:17).

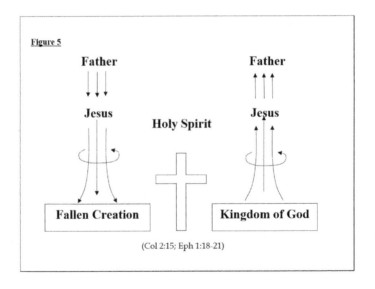

Figure 5

Father   Father

Jesus   Holy Spirit   Jesus

Fallen Creation   Kingdom of God

(Col 2:15; Eph 1:18-21)

So it is then, that the cross and its authority is now ours to wield (Mark 16:17,18) for the continuing purpose of Jesus: "...to destroy the devil's work" (1 John 3:8). This is illustrated in Figure 5.

Armed with this authority, informed with understanding of God's plan, equipped with our God-given spiritual weapons and assured by Jesus' assertion that our enemy's defences will not be able to withstand the onslaught of His Church, one may be excused for thinking a mere century of focussed combat would be more than sufficient to overthrow one angelic usurper and his finite band of demonic followers... Not so! For the past two millennia the Church has been carrying a commission with which she has been largely loathe or lax to engage. Perhaps, even more tragically, she has been entirely ignorant of it, or bent on pursuing a different commission for her own purposes and advancement. So, what's gone wrong?

Questions for further consideration: (Chapters 4 – 7)

a) What does Isaiah 9:6 say about the Trinity?
b) When compared with Isaiah 14:12-15, what does Satan's temptation of Eve in Genesis 3:5b reveal about himself, and his motivations?
c) What character qualities of God would you expect to see visible in a practical manifestation of the kingdom of God?

d) If we are to engage Satan and his forces with spiritual weapons, what are these weapons?
e) In what ways have you exercised your "cross-given" authority over the enemies of God?

Chapter 8

The Two Gospels

In Acts 19:3 Paul discovers a group of Ephesian disciples and has cause to ask them, "which baptism did you receive?" Perhaps a similar question to be addressed to today's church members could be phrased, "which gospel did you believe?" There are two gospels and I would like to explain the difference.

First of all, there is the classic gospel of salvation by faith. Entirely Scriptural and beloved of preachers these centuries past, this proclaims God's merciful and gracious appeal to a humanity which naturally deserves nothing better than outright damnation. It may be summarised along the following lines:

- All have rebelled against God and have engaged in wrongdoing. These are a natural expression of our fallen, sinful inner nature, which deserves judgement resulting in eternal damnation.
- Out of God's enduring love for humanity, He offers us a chance to be freed from our sinful inner compulsions, to receive His very own presence within us as our new inner nature, and to exchange our future hellish prospect for a heavenly eternity of rejoicing in His blissful company.

- This possibility has been achieved by Jesus when He died at Calvary: He took the punishment due to us, symbolically taking our old sinful natures, (our inescapable capacity for wrongdoing), to the grave. He demonstrated the effectiveness of this through His resurrection.
- We can now appropriate these benefits for ourselves by making a personal choice, based on faith alone to:
  - contritely confess our wrongs and ask God's forgiveness
  - repent, or turn away, from our lifestyle of rebelling against God's ways
  - ask Jesus to include us in His Calvary transaction
  - welcome Holy Spirit, as the presence of God, to take up residence within us together with His new nature
  - look forward with confidence to our own resurrection, after the example of Jesus, and to a heavenly eternity in the presence of God.

By responding positively to this message of hope, literally billions of men and women have received their own salvation as Father God has "rescued us from the dominion of darkness and brought us into the kingdom of the Son he loves, in whom we have redemption, the forgiveness of sins" (Colossians 1:13,14).

We are further assured in 1 John 1:9 that "if we confess our sins, he [God] is faithful and just and will forgive us our sins and purify us from all unrighteousness". This gospel I have preached for over forty years - in churches, in schools, on the streets and in workshops - and for this I am most grateful. For ease of identification later on, I want to denote this as the "Gospel of the Cross", in that it has the saving work of the cross as its focus and triumph.

Now, there is another gospel...

This "other" gospel is, again, entirely Scriptural. It would have caused Paul no problems irrespective of his commitment to "preach Christ crucified" (1 Corinthians 1:23). It was preached by none other than Jesus Himself and those disciples whom He appointed on occasions to partner in His preaching work during His earthly ministry (Luke 9:2; Luke 10:9). In fact, apart from oblique references to how "the Son of Man must be lifted up" (John 3:14,15), Jesus does not actually preach the "Gospel of the Cross". Instead, Jesus preaches another gospel: the "Gospel of the Kingdom".

This Gospel (or "Good News") of the Kingdom begins with and incorporates all of what we have termed the Gospel of the Cross. However, it is much more expansive in its scope and goes further still than the personal benefits which the resurrection brings to each of us. Jesus is, of course, concerned that all should be saved into a new, life-giving active relationship with Himself. However, there is more. He is equally concerned that these new, remade lives should be fruitfully engaged in the spiritual battle to build, or rebuild, God's kingdom on Earth. This longing and expectation of God is very much rooted in the practical. It is not some symbolic hope for mere intellectual assent where we all agree that the kingdom of God on earth is a good idea in principle. Instead, it should produce a tangible demonstration from us of God's love for His creation, causing us to shout His compassion and purpose for people the world over.

I remember hearing an apocryphal story of a professor in the field of child psychology. He continually angered his neighbours by chanting, "That's not the way; that's not the way! Love is the way; love is the way!" whenever he saw parents shouting correction at their children. One day, when his driveway had just been freshly concreted, a neighbour's child rode his bicycle through the still wet surface. This left deep wheel ruts in the smoothed finish of the concrete. Enraged, the professor pulled the boy off his bike and began smacking him. A neighbour happened to be passing, and seizing the opportunity began shouting, "That's not the way; that's not the way! Love is the way; love is the way!" "Madam", the professor responded, "I do love him, but I love Him in the abstract, and not in the concrete!" Tragically, for countless millions God's love for humanity remains in the abstract, because His Church has largely failed to demonstrate the enormity of His love in the concrete - failed to seriously engage in building His kingdom of peace, justice, health, wholeness, compassion and kindness, and all the other holy qualities emanating from the character of God.

However, it should be noted that there have been flashes of brilliance illuming the darkness of centuries past. The latter part of the Eighteenth Century saw Britain deeply socially divided, with some in a state of abject poverty and others living in landed depravity. Parliament was disinterested in the lot of the common man but operated more as an elite club for the benefit and continuing prosperity of the few. For the majority of the population, conditions were bad and may well have found a remedy not too dissimilar to that of the French Revolution. This, but for the rise of Christian Evangelicalism[15]. It has been argued that a corresponding "British Revolution" was avoided by the subsequent soul-winning fervour and emphasis on personal holiness promoted by this movement, and which was perhaps best typified by, and which fuelled the preaching of John Wesley, George Whitfield and their adherents. Certainly, they changed the spiritual temperature of Britain.

This rising tide of evangelicalism brought with it not only a hunger for souls to be reconciled to God, but also for a society transformed. Stephen Tomkins, in his book "The Clapham Sect" writes that, "...evangelicals were creatures of the Enlightenment and so believed that God gave us a

---

[15] "Evangelicanism" here relates to the movement, originating in the mid-18th Century, characterised by spiritual fervour, passionate prayer, Spirit-filled, soul-winning mission and the promotion of righteousness in daily living. Its foundations include the authority and reliability of Biblical truth, the necessity for a spiritual conversion experience to know God personally, the centrality of the saving death and resurrection of Jesus Christ to Christian faith and a responsibility to share and demonstrate the gospel message in loving, compassionate activity. It is used here distinct from any subsequent connotations through which the word has been usurped for political appeal and advancement, or to identify a political sub-set.

world to be improved, not just conserved"[16]. These reborn Christians committed themselves to serving the marginalised and disenfranchised, compelled by the Love of God at work in them (2 Cor 5:14). Perhaps most notable of the Clapham Sect's cultural transformations was the abolition of the slave trade in Britain; initiated by Quakers in North America, and working with a wide variety of campaigners[17], the cause was most famously championed to its conclusion in the British Parliament by William Wilberforce. This, however, was not their sole effort in transforming society. They had equally focussed campaigns to improve the conditions and prospects of the chronically poor, including releasing tens of thousands of small debtors and their families from foetid prisons, promoting literacy through Sunday Schools and countering rampant vice and immorality in Georgian Britain.

There are many stories to tell of Christian activism and reformation from British history: Elizabeth Fry and John Howard were highly influential in penal reform; the Earl of

---

[16] p. 19.

[17] The abolition of slavery in Britain was a long, complex road with many people fighting side by side, including many with personal experience of slavery. Notable in this regard, amongst others, were Mary Prince, the first woman to present an anti-slavery petition in Parliament, Olaudah Equiano, whose autobiography exposed the horrors of slavery, and Ottobah Cugoano who, in 1797, published a book arguing against the "...Evil and Wicked Traffic..." of slavery. All were significant contributions to the passing of the Slave Trade Act of 1807, as indeed were the efforts of the Sons of Africa campaigning group.

Shaftsbury campaigned to improve children's working conditions, for the reform of public health and the treatment of those judged insane; the Cadbury family stood against animal cruelty, promoted adult education and made improvements in housing conditions, employee welfare and labour relations. The resulting social transformation produced a society able to embrace the upheaval of the Industrial Revolution without descending into further anarchy. It additionally laid a foundation upon which later generations could build a new society. Whilst this new Victorian society was far from perfect, it did nevertheless provide a platform where righteousness was not ridiculed and serving the needs of the marginalised was applauded. Whilst opportunity to build God's kingdom in fullness was not seized in this instance, the advances achieved by those committed to seeing God's kingdom come on earth in a concrete way is significant.

These cultural transformations occurred through the God-inspired activation of women and men who loved Him and were compelled to see the kingdom come to earth. Some were in positions of huge influence and power - politicians, bankers, civil servants, aristocrats, lawyers, teachers, military officers and clergymen – many others worked and prayed with less influence on the earth, but just as much in the heavens: but they were all committed to transforming a nation in the name of Jesus. God may yet seek to elevate His people to positions of secular influence, "for such a time as this" (Esther 4:14). Indeed, He has done and is doing so. But how can the Church be ready to seize this opportunity?

The Gospel of the Cross is a powerful and true word. It rightly declares, "God made you; God loves you; God died for you; God saves you". This might be represented on our diagram as a broad sweep from creation to the cross. The particular inadequacy of this message lies not in anything lacking from its truth, but rather that the message stops at personal salvation.

The Gospel of the Kingdom has a crucial, life-changing element to add: "God made you; God loves you; God died for you; God saves you; God has got a purpose for your life!" And the purpose? "Build the kingdom!"

The "Come to Jesus" appeal of the Gospel of the Cross can infer the sub-text, "and come into the church to be safe until He returns". It is as though having enrolled into the fellowship of believers – the "army" of God – and having been issued with our uniform, we are then escorted to a comfy chair, provided with a newspaper and slippers, and advised to remain so until our Commanding Officer calls us home!

In contrast, the Gospel of the Kingdom speaks, "Come to Jesus, and go out and transform the world into His likeness!" For this is a gospel of purpose and of power. It regards salvation not as an end in itself, but rather the new and focussed beginning of a holy, Jesus-given campaign, in which we all have a part to play. We are commissioned, even expected, to bear fruit to affect material change and progress towards God's kingdom goal. Ample parables of Jesus illustrate this point, but how is this to be achieved?

Questions for further consideration:

a) How and when did you respond to the Gospel of the Cross?
b) How do you practically demonstrate God's love among the community where you live?
c) What areas of society do you feel called to redeem?
d) How have you impacted the secular world for God's kingdom within your sphere of influence thus far?

Chapter 9

Building God's Kingdom

"All the world's a stage", declares Jacques in Shakespeare's play "As you like it". However, I find greater depth and truth, although admittedly a little less poetry, in the cry, "All the world's a building site!" And we, the Church, are the builders. Unfortunately, our building site is not clear, virgin land. It is already full of structures and systems which are well established despite their tendency to hurt and imprison people, as well as accommodate them. There are dividing walls, unholy habits and social structures to be broken down, as well as new structures to be built founded on God's character. There are two distinctly different building sites where we are told to build God's kingdom.

The first is "within" us, internally, as indicated by Jesus in Luke's gospel:

> "Once, having been asked by the Pharisees when the kingdom of God would come, Jesus replied, 'The kingdom of God does not come with your careful observation, nor will people say, 'Here it is', or 'There it is', because the kingdom of God is within you'" (Luke 17:20-21).

If God's kingdom is wherever the rule and reign of God is manifest, then God's kingdom within represents a life wholly submitted to and under the direction of the ways of God. Many will recognise this as the goal of discipleship, albeit a process.

The second location in which God requires His kingdom to be built is, conversely, "without" our beings. The aim is to conform society's values and structures to His likeness and design. To this end were the messages of many Old Testament prophets directed[18], a selection of which are worth quoting at length:

> "You who turn justice into bitterness and cast righteousness to the ground...you hate the one who reproves in court and despise him who tells the truth. You trample on the poor and force them to give you grain. Therefore, though you have stone mansions, you will not live in them: though you have planted lush vineyards, you will not drink their wine. For I know how many are your offences and how great your sins. You oppress the righteous and take bribes and you deprive the poor of justice at the courts... Hate evil, love good; maintain justice in the courts" (Amos 5:7-15).

> "Stand up, plead your case before the mountains; let the hills hear what you have to say... And what does

---

[18] It is worth referring to the entire chapters of Amos 5, Micah 6 and Isaiah 58.

the Lord require of you? To act justly and to love mercy and to walk humbly with your God... Shall I acquit a man with dishonest scales, with a bag of false weights? Her rich men are violent; her people are liars and their tongues speak deceitfully. Therefore, I have begun to destroy you, to ruin you because of your sins" (Micah 6:1,8,11-13).

"Shout it aloud, do not hold back, raise your voice like a trumpet. Declare to my people their rebellion and to the house of Jacob their sins... on the day of your fasting, you do as you please and exploit all your workers. Is not this the kind of fasting I have chosen: to loose the chains of injustice and untie the cords of the yoke, to set the oppressed free and break every yoke? Is it not to share your food with the hungry and to provide the poor wanderer with shelter – when you see the naked, to clothe him, and not to turn away from your own flesh and blood?" (Isaiah 58:1,3,6,7).

The words of the prophets repeatedly speak out against the exploitation of the poor, injustice in the legal system and unrighteous business, pronouncing God's anger against those within Israel who aligned with or failed to overturn corruption. We have at times found the Church replicating this prophetic model and confronting unrighteousness and injustice in society, although there have been times and seasons when it has amounted to little more than shouting through our church windows at "those out there".

Confronting and overturning injustice, exploitation and unrighteousness is unlikely to be effectively achieved from the security of our churches, the reassurance of our "comfy chairs", and from behind our "newspapers" filled with matters of absorbing ecclesiastical interest! Change is built. Forward progress on both building sites of "within" and "without" requires an active Church - but the latter case demands hands on involvement by the Church out in society: among the politicians, the educators, the artists, the scientists, the families, the business and justice machineries of our nations.

This is not to say that only those with professional qualifications can hope to bear kingdom fruit in changing our society, and that they alone should bear the blame for our society's moral deterioration. The truth is that it is "our" society. The entire church, with all of her members, must accept some responsibility for what "we" have made it. The values of our society are not determined solely by our elected leaders: the rank and file of a nation has a far more extensive role to play than merely through the ballot box. Society is that which we live out day by day, and the sum of what we put into it. Society is formed in our parliaments and during school gate conversations; it is formed during workshop antics and attitudes demonstrated towards fellow workers; it is shaped by marital fidelity, or otherwise; in championing fairness on the playing field – or at the tax office; it forms in the decision to refuse to accept pornography - however "soft" - as harmless, and in demonstrating to the many who are watching from the wings that integrity and enjoyment are not mutually exclusive strangers. Society is the sum of its parts: growing out of the day-to-day interactions and decisions of those who live it out, of what is collectively agreed as 'normal', what is resisted and accepted.

Thus, our churches should be speaking and demonstrating God's better blueprint for our daily living at every level, rising to embrace this corporate task with excitement and relish. However, the blatant betrayals by those within our churches of its own standards, especially when holding positions of leadership, have lamentably eroded the platform upon which the institution of the established church could once stand and speak authoritatively into matters of national life. Pronouncements by members of church hierarchy to a now-secularised society are at best regarded as irrelevancies, or at worst as arcane, bigoted and arrogant hypocrisies. In either case, they are unwelcome! What's more, the prevailing scorn with which such pronouncements are greeted undermines the courageous example and efforts of Christians who are living out "kingdom" values as salt in their communities. The nett result is that the church is often ineffective in building God's kingdom ways in society.

In contrast, churches in some Southern hemisphere cultures, choose largely to avoid interaction with the worlds of politics, commerce and entertainment; these spheres are regarded as being altogether too ungodly for her involvement without compromising her sanctification. Reluctance to engage in some of these streams of society may have been handed down as part of a denomination's culture. Alternatively, it may be regarded as a useful control mechanism by leaders to keep their congregations in a manageable state, or perhaps be a knee jerk reaction to past or currently observed sinful excesses.

Perhaps the best results achieved by the established church in creating social change have been seen in South America. However, other factors such as Liberation Theology and a strong received culture founded on Roman Catholic values have contributed to some successes here. This could be the subject of a further, separate study elsewhere. Additionally, some church members impacted by the renewal movement in Latino cultures have similarly brought significant kingdom influence to their own particular communities, cities or spheres of activity, and examples may be found scattered through the writings of Ed Silvoso[19].

Ultimately, there is a common pattern or tendency for societies around the globe to slip towards corruption, and to compromise the often high ideals from which they were born. Wisdom tells us that "through the blessing of the upright a city is exalted" (Proverbs 11:11a) and "righteousness exalts a nation" (Proverbs 13:34); it is perhaps little wonder that the converse can be so readily and near-universally observed. Unrighteousness is a recognisable and international pandemic which wreaks a

---

[19] A number of such examples are included in Ed Silvoso's book "Transformation" – see the "Bibliography" appendix herein.

terrible loss of life year after year. And righteousness is the key if any "kingdom" building work is to be done.

Questions for further consideration:

a) To what extent is God ruling and reigning over your thoughts, actions, hopes and dreams, lifestyle and finances?
b) Do you think the Church should withdraw or engage with society?
c) How have you sought to engage with society in the past?

Chapter 10

Getting Righteousness Right

Let's return to expand upon our consideration of the Gospel of the Cross (see Chapter 8), and the wider, all embracing good news of the Gospel of the Kingdom.

The Gospel of the Cross is undoubtedly a Message of Salvation; emphasised by the Western Church through which a personal response reaps a change in personal condition and status. As an individual repents from their own way, declares that Jesus is Lord over their life and commits to follow Him, various transactions take place, including salvation from eternal damnation and the indwelling of the person of the Holy Spirit, who comes to reside within them as a guarantee of all that is to come (Ephesians 1:13,14). This salvation cannot be earned in any way by our own merits but is a free gift from God to all who choose to receive it. It is an act of grace on His part, undeserved favour towards us, as Paul explains:

> "For it is by grace you have been saved, through faith – and this is not from ourselves, it is the gift of God – not by works, so that no-one can boast" (Ephesians 2:8-9).

Consequently, none can demand this salvation as a deserved right, rather forgiveness and salvation are for those who approach God with humility rather than the presumption of pride (Psalm 18:27; Psalm 149:4) and:

> "…if my people, who are called by my name, will humble themselves and pray and seek my face and turn from their wicked ways, then I will hear from heaven and will forgive their sin and will heal their land" (2 Chronicles 7:14).

This humility was the heart attitude demonstrated by Jesus, who,

> "…being found in appearance as a man, he humbled himself and became obedient to death – even death on a cross!" (Philippians 2:8).

It is the example we are commended to follow:

> "Your attitude should be the attitude as that of Christ Jesus…" (Philippians 2:5).

and which releases the grace of God to us,

> "Young men, in the same way be submissive to those who are older. All of you, clothe yourselves with humility towards one another, because, 'God opposes the proud, but gives grace to the humble.' Humble yourselves, therefore, under God's mighty

hand, that he may lift you up in due time" (1 Peter 5:5-6).

Thus, we experience the salvation offered by the Gospel of the Cross by walking through the "Doorway of Grace" with a "Heart of Humility" (See Figure 6).

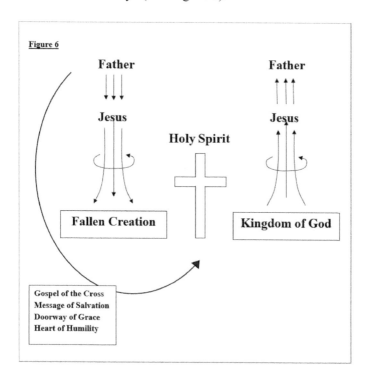

Figure 6

The Gospel of the Kingdom is a message which extends the free provision of personal salvation from the damaging effects of sin, going further in proclaiming the future transformation of all that is and redeeming it back to its original design under God. It foresees nothing less than a physical fulfilment of Jesus' prayer, "thy kingdom come…in earth as it is in heaven" (Matthew 6:10).

As such, the Gospel of the Kingdom is rightly termed a "Message of Transformation" and this was the intended thrust of the four gospel writers from the beginning. Jesus came to "seek and to save that which was lost" (Luke 19:10). This is normally taken to refer to people, but Jesus' salvation mandate reaches to a far grander scale, announcing and initiating the establishing of God's kingdom. This was the beginning of a revolution: an invasion of worldly systems and structures by heaven's agents so as to bring the likeness and patterns of our eternal Father to permeate and predominate the earth. This was understood by the gospel writers as the dramatic fulfilment by Jesus of God's prophesied, long-time purposes for Israel. The scale of the message was always global. Its intended effect: earth shattering. Its goal: the transformation of all things!

That such a global, all-encompassing message has been diluted to "join our club and try to be good" is a tragedy. We have to own again the enormity of God's intended transformation process. Each is invited to participate in this process. Each is invited to embrace God's greater purpose. Each is invited to be active to advance and enact His kingdom through the power of the Spirit and the leading of the Shephard. Everyone has a part to play, irrespective of circumstance or position in society. His goal is not merely to "improve things a bit", "make things better", nor even "change things around". I believe His goal is nothing short of "Transformation". After all, He is not the god of "that'll do", but the Author of the "very good" (Genesis 1:31). But who are those who will build and be a part of His glorious new kingdom?

God is very clear in His Word that His kingdom is tied to righteousness. Not "trying to be a decent enough sort of person" goodness, but righteousness. On this matter we need to be very careful to clearly communicate the truth of the gospel message concerning righteousness. Historically, great confusion has been sown by some, insisting that "doing good things" is, by itself, sufficient to qualify one for entrance into God's heavenly kingdom. This performance-based route to acceptance by God is completely opposed to the principles He expounds in His Word. We read in Isaiah 64:6 that "...all our righteous acts are like filthy rags...", and in Romans 3 Paul, when quoting verses from Psalm 14, concludes by affirming that no-one will be declared righteous by their own efforts of trying to meet the demands of God's standards. So, this "kingdom-orientated righteousness" under consideration here is *not* achieved by trying to do good things in our own strength, in the manner that a well-meaning non-Christian may do. Out of His grace, God provides to us an altogether different mechanism or process which works to affect this righteousness in us, and this will be explained in our subsequent chapters. Notwithstanding this, some verses on the matter can appear a little alarming at first. Jesus told His disciples, that compared to the Pharisees who were, in their day, righteousness fanatics:

> "For I tell you that unless your righteousness surpasses that of the Pharisees and the teachers of the law, you will certainly not enter the kingdom of (God)" (Matthew 5:20). (Parentheses mine).

However, the extreme error of the Pharisees was that they were pursuing righteousness through the Law, which produces self-righteousness and a religious spirit. In contrast, the call for the kingdom-building follower of Jesus is to pursue righteousness through grace and humility. In fact, the pursuit of *His* righteousness, (not our self-righteousness, but the righteousness that comes through Jesus), and *His* Kingdom, are inextricably linked:

> "But seek first his kingdom and his righteousness, and all these things will be given to you as well" (Matthew 6:33).

It is those who have the righteousness of Jesus who will inherit the kingdom and enjoy its benefits. In the parable of the sheep and the goats, we can see the connection between those who enter the kingdom and the "righteous".

> "Then the king will say to those on his right, 'Come, you who are blessed by my Father; take your inheritance, the kingdom prepared for you since the creation of the world'" (Matthew 25:34).

"Then the righteous will answer him, "Lord when did we see you hungry and feed you, or thirsty and gave you something to drink?" (Matthew 25:37).

Jesus reveals further insight in His parable about the kingdom of God which He likens to a wedding banquet. The king's desire to fill the banquet causes him to extend his invitation to common people who are "both good and bad" – all are free to accept. However, the king's meeting with those who have accepted culminates with one guest being forcibly ejected from the banquet (the kingdom), as evidenced in the concluding verses of the story, as follows;

"So, the servants went out into the streets and gathered all the people they could find, both good and bad, and the wedding hall was filled with guests. But when the king came in to see the guests, he noticed a man there who was not wearing wedding clothes. 'Friend,' he asked, 'how did you get in here without wearing wedding clothes?' The man was speechless. Then the king told the attendants, 'Tie him hand and foot, and throw him outside into the darkness where there will be weeping and gnashing of teeth. For many are invited, but few are chosen'" (Matthew 22:10-14).

The guest not wearing wedding clothes is thrown "...outside in the darkness...", a seemingly severe consequence for transgressing a dress code. However, the key to understanding the importance of the wedding clothes is found in Revelation 19:7-8. At the "Wedding of the Lamb" the wedding clothes of fine linen, in which the Bride is clad, represent "the righteous acts of the saints". So here again, acceptance and remaining in God's kingdom is consequent upon righteousness.

This emphasis can be somewhat uncomfortable because, as intimated earlier, it can be distorted to sound like "good works get you into the kingdom". Nevertheless, this message goes back to the very beginning of Jesus' ministry. He opened His preaching in Matthew 4:17 with nothing more spectacular than just repeating the message His cousin John was already proclaiming, as seen in Matthew 3:2. It was a message of repentance to righteousness "…for the kingdom of (God) is near" (parentheses mine). It was a call for preparation so as to be able to enter God's new dominion and would be seen to bear fruit in due course. This effectiveness can be gauged from Jesus' word:

> "…Jesus said to them, 'I tell you the truth, the tax collectors and the prostitutes are entering the kingdom of God ahead of you. For John came to you to show you the way of righteousness, and you did not believe him, but the tax collectors and the prostitutes did. And even after you saw this you did not repent and believe him'" (Matthew 21:31-32).

From this, we see even the tax collectors and prostitutes who embraced John's way of righteousness were entering the kingdom of God ahead of the religious leaders of the day. So, just to be certain, how do we get this righteousness?

God is the giver of good gifts to His children, and righteousness is no exception to this rule. Whilst we do not deserve to enjoy this stain-free state, it freely comes by faith along with our salvation when we first believe.

> "But now a righteousness from God, apart from the Law, has been made known, to which the Law and the Prophets testify. This righteousness from God comes through faith in Jesus Christ to all who believe…" (Romans 3:21,22).

However, having received this righteousness, can we now sit back with complacency, trusting in an assumed immunity from censure in the face of wilful future disobedience? This uncomfortable question receives further credibility in Galatians 5:19-21, where Paul lists numerous "acts of the sinful nature" and announces that "those who live like this will not inherit the kingdom of God".

> "The acts of the sinful nature are obvious: sexual immorality, impurity and debauchery; idolatry and witchcraft; hatred, discord, jealousy, fits of rage, selfish ambition, dissentions, factions and envy; drunkenness, orgies, and the like. I warn you, as I did before, that those who live like this will not inherit the kingdom of God" (Galatians 5:19-21).

It must be remembered here that Paul is writing this letter to a church, not the local den of iniquity. But, happily, there is no entrance examination nor behavioural threshold which must be satisfied before one can attach to a church congregation. This does, however, mean that church gatherings can comprise a rather "mixed bag" of people, amongst whom some of the above excesses may indeed still feature in their everyday lives. It is all very reminiscent of Jesus' parable about the wheat and the weeds, (Matthew 13:24-30 and 36-43), where that which is good and that which is bad are allowed to grow together until the time of harvest. Such can be a snapshot of many "mixed" church congregations, and Paul's message is as relevant today as when first written almost 2,000 years ago. It serves as a timely warning to true believers, members of the *ekklesia*, not to let slip their focus, nor compromise their commitment to Jesus and His ways. Ultimately, it is the principle expounded by James, (in James 2:18), which provides the ruling maxim in this matter. While James explains that it is the outworking of genuine faith that produces good works, so it is that our living, vital and ongoing relationship with Jesus that sustains our righteousness. Even so, lifestyle choices, even by Christians, invoke consequences. Let us take notice of these things.

A subtle, but serious, trap which the church faces in this is to persuade herself that she's doing better than she actually is. It is a very dangerous deception. A friend had a dream which helped him understand how God sees the church in relation to righteousness. Looking down, and very close to where he stood, was a line drawn in the sand which he knew to represent God's righteous standard. Excited by how close he was to achieving this, he could almost touch the line with his feet, he was congratulating himself on how well he was doing. Then he heard a voice... He immediately recognised this to be the voice of God, who asked, "What line is that? That's not my line; you've drawn that line". In his dream my friend replied, "Oh, where's your line then?" "Look up", said God, "there is my line" and in the far distance, a long way off from where he was standing, lay another line in the sand. As my friend continued to watch this line it began to rotate from the horizontal into the vertical plane, whereupon it changed from a line into a man. And the man was Jesus.

God's standard, or template, of righteousness is not a list of rules, but a Man. Jesus has fleshed out an example of God's pattern for us and explained that righteousness flows out of a right heart attitude (Matthew chapters 5-7). In fact, if we want to flesh out the detail of what righteousness looks like, we have no further to look than these three chapters of Matthew's gospel. They might be regarded as Jesus' "Righteousness Manifesto". Our goal in righteousness, as in so many other things, is to be like Jesus.

So then, in so far as our diagram is concerned, entrance into the kingdom of God may now be reckoned to be through a "Doorway of Righteousness".

It is worth reminding ourselves at this point that in this matter of righteousness we must resist comparison; we have no right to judge the performance of others against our own.

We have a tendency to looking on the exterior. God sees the heart (1 Sam 16:7), and righteousness flows out of a heart attitude. Secondly, we can never fully appreciate the depths of God's grace. We are often too quick to condemn the errors and weaknesses of others whilst glossing over or minimizing our own: judging ourselves against our intentions and others by their actions. God encourages us to first face our own shortcomings, and then helps us to rise and ultimately triumph over these challenges. There is infinite grace for the working out of our salvation. Peter heard Jesus say that, "…whoever acknowledges me before men, the Son of Man will also acknowledge Him before the angels of God. But he who disowns me before men will be disowned before the angels of God" (Luke 12:8-9). Peter does indeed disown Jesus (Luke 22:54-62) and is later restored and recommissioned by Jesus (John 21:15-17). Who then, dare pronounce limits to God's matchless grace?

Even so, having received a new righteousness from God at conversion, let us now pursue this as an active lifestyle if we want to continue in righteousness. The question now arises as to how we can be expected to achieve this. If we are indeed to be like Jesus in these things, our fleshly weakness and sometime appetite for wrongful ways may shout "Impossible!" to this goal. However, God has, again, provided a way by which we may aspire to this end, and, no surprises – love is the way!

Questions for further consideration:

a) Does the idea of "Transformation" fill you with longing or with uncertainty?

b) Do you find "Righteousness" to be a positive word, or one with uncomfortable associations, and if so, why?

c) How complacent do you think our churches have become regarding righteousness?

d) How do you define righteousness?

e) How important to you personally is living righteously?

f) By how much do you think it fine to infringe God's standard of righteousness?

Chapter 11

"Love is the Way"

A popular song from 1960's Britain declared that "Love is all around". Coming from a certainly secular standpoint, this sentiment holds a lot of spiritual truth! For if we were ever able to "see" the foundations upon which all existence is built, a common platform upon which the universe has, does and will continue to stand and function, then "Love" would be there. How can we be so sure of this? Because the universe is not only the exquisite brainchild of Father God, but also His "heartchild"; a tangible expression of Himself – both the fruit and object of His love in one. And, as recorded in 1 John 4:8,16, "God *is* love"! It's as though He just can't help Himself loving, and He lavishes this love upon our world, (John 3:16):

> "For God *so* loved the world that he gave his one and only Son, that whoever believes in him shall not perish but have eternal life."

There is much that has been, and will yet be, written in praise of love in its various manifestations. Here, however, I want to direct our attention not so much to "Love" itself as an object, but rather to what "Love" produces – its bi-products if you will.

Primary among the bi-products of God's love, for us in this instance, must be the love which is consequently engendered in our hearts as human beings. Referring to God, John writes that, "We love because he first loved us", (1 John 4:19). Our ability to love is happily inbuilt within each of us, evidencing in whose image we have been created. Furthermore, our love for God as Christians is a fitting and irrepressible response when we come to understand the enormity of His love for us, and what sacrificial extravagance His love unleashed toward us. Naturally, I write of God's ceaseless, loving pursuit of relationship with mankind, and His ultimate coming personally in the form of Jesus to redeem us with His own suffering. As singer-songwriter Graham Kendrick penned, "Hands that flung stars into space (were) to cruel nails surrendered", (my inclusion in parentheses). This really is love beyond our wildest dreams, and it is this love with which we are enwrapped by God. It cries out for a response. In similar vein, I recall a story concerning a young man, raised in a strong Christian family to follow the ways of God, but who chose to turn his back on all of this with vigour. His parents, (whom I know), were heartbroken, but in the fullness of time he did indeed repent and return, reaffirming his love for Jesus and stepping into church leadership. When asked how this had become possible, the father replied, "We just kept loving him unconditionally, because in the end you can't keep kicking against love forever!" It's all so reminiscent of the "Prodigal Son" parable[20] – one that I prefer to call the "Parable of the

---

[20] Luke 15:11-32

Running Father" as it refocuses our attention onto God's passion for us. This is the sort of love that demands a response.

So then, what does, (or should), our loving response look like?

From the well-known words of John 3:16 we can easily recognise that love wants to give. So, among the desires included in a loving response to God should be a desire to give pleasure to Him and not to cause Him pain. That God can and does feel pain may be a strange idea for some, but this is clearly demonstrated in Genesis 6:5,6:

> "The LORD saw how great man's wickedness on the earth had become, and that every inclination of the thoughts of his heart was only evil all the time. The LORD was grieved that he had made man on the earth, and his heart was filled with pain."

From the above we see one source of God's pain is our sinful inclinations, and consequently, love demands that we address these. Here, then, is the genesis of one of the great themes of the Old Testament: righteousness – living in a sin-free condition. God's desire for this is expressed in Leviticus 19:2 when speaking to Israel;

> "...Be holy because I, the LORD your God, am holy."

And in order to flesh out what this entailed, we were given The Law as our guide. Unfortunately, what was to communicate God's heart was received by many as His exclusive list of regulations, the perfect observance of which was beyond the capability of Israel. To do better in this department, help was needed.

Now God was always mindful of this, and out of His love for us He always intended to intervene in this predicament at the right time. Enter Jesus! And so Jesus, the Lamb of God, became the sacrifice who took upon Himself the consequences of all our wrongdoing, and reopened the opportunity for us humans to again enjoy a close, personal, conscious relationship with God. As already described in Chapter 8, availing ourselves of this reconnection with our Creator demands a purposeful decision to this end on our part. Furthermore, once this divine transformation is initiated, then we receive a "righteousness from God (which) comes by faith", (Romans 3:22, parentheses mine). However, the concern now is how to *continue* to live righteously without sliding interminably back into old habit patterns, hurtful to God.

In 1 Corinthians 11:1 Paul advises his readers to follow his example, as he follows the example of Christ. This practice of following the example of Jesus, or imitating His lifestyle, appears to have been very successfully embraced throughout the Early Church, evidenced by the nickname given to the adherents of this new religion sweeping through the world of the New Testament: "Christians". The root of this word is actually "Little Christs", and what perhaps was intended as a scornful jibe could indeed be worn as a badge of honour by believers, attesting to their measure of success in imitating Christ. But if Israel had so signally and repeatedly failed to meet God's lifestyle requirements throughout the Old Testament narratives, how could these New Testament believers achieve what was previously impossible?

Under the Law, as seen particularly in the attitudes and pronouncements of the gospel Pharisees, righteousness was being driven from the outside into people's behaviour. A thankless pursuit, chasing a perfection beyond reach. However, through having had our relationship with God restored through Jesus' atonement, we can now enjoy His very presence within each of us, in the Person of His Spirit. Thus, through this internal relationship, the life of Jesus can now be released from the inside outwards in our behaviour. This is no longer "imitation through exertion", but rather "imitation through habitation". A work of pure genius and grace on God's part and all an outworking of God's love… (This mechanism receives further attention in Chapter 12).

Now beyond our desire to live lives which are stain free, another means by which we can give loving response to God is to share His passion for His purposes. When we consider how good and how wise are God's purposes, then it is only natural that we should want to see their fulfilment. The astounding truth that He invites us to partner with Him in this only adds to the richness of our engaging with Him in these matters.

Amongst other interests I am an avid enthusiast of railways. I find their history, their engineering, their operation, social impact and future development fascinating. One avenue through which this interest, or passion, is expressed is that of travelling by train and collecting train numbers – a hobby popularly known as "trainspotting" and an unbroken pursuit now of my past 65 years. A considerable joy to me has been the similar interest and adoption of this hobby by our three grandsons. Together we have journeyed by rail all around the United Kingdom for many years now, enjoying each others' company and, in the process, ever deepening the bonds which we share. Their continued appetite for these occasions has, for me, been nothing less than a tangible expression of their love for a grandad and his sometime idiosyncratic pursuits.

Ultimately, it all comes down to love: "Because I love you, I want to see your passions realised and your purposes fulfilled", and in God's particular case here – it's His kingdom! We long to see His kingdom established, in reality – now!

Continuing with this theme, yet another way in which we can respond to God's love is to give Him our obedience. In past times and in some strains of thinking God is an austere, distant figure making extensive demands upon us poor humans, and requiring of us enduring sacrificial feats of obedience to prove our commitment to Him. This could not be further from the truth. Our intended obedience to God is not some slavish submission required by a cruel despot, but rather that of a much-loved child wanting to please a doting parent. Such obedience is first of all a response to God's love instead of a requirement of His holiness. Having stated this, it should not be reckoned as an optional extra to be casually rendered to God, or not, depending on our mood. This is a matter for serious consideration because, as we will see in our following chapter, God takes obedience seriously. The same can also be said about righteousness, and indeed obedience and righteousness are inextricably linked, bound together and inseparable from relationship with God, and only possible through our relationship with Him.

A regular and unwelcome comment by teachers on school reports of a generation past was, "Must do better!" To be honest, it's a bit of a withering judgement bringing deflation and deepening despair to a child instead of inspiring improvement. While we can also sometimes be guilty of speaking these words to ourselves, this is not God's way. For He is the One who overwhelms us with encouragement, who binds up our wounds and disappointments, who covers our sins with His love and who lifts us and carries us when overburdened. This is His love in practical reality. He is the parent who says to the struggling child, "I believe in you: we can do this together. Let me do what you can't, just trust me, for when you come to the end of your own ability, it is me, through my love, that has a way".

Once we know God, it is no hard thing, no sacrifice, to abandon ourselves to the love He has for us. It becomes no hardship to choose to walk in His way.

Questions for further consideration:

a) How convinced are you that God really loves you?
b) How do you respond to the love of others, and how does this compare with your response to God's love for you?
c) If you have tried "being good", (according to The Law), how successful have you been?
d) How have you found Holy Spirit's indwelling presence to be helpful in pleasing God through your behaviour?

Chapter 12

Walk This Way

A key principle for understanding how to pursue righteousness is found in Romans 6:16: "...obedience leads to righteousness". It is perhaps impossible to overstate the importance of obedience in the catalogue of Christian imperatives. If Jesus' first heart cry in the Lord's Prayer was for God's kingdom to come, then His second was for obedience, "...Your will be done on earth as it is in heaven" (Matthew 6:10). Over and over again we find Jesus emphasising the centrality of obedience:

- as an evidence of our love for Him (John 14:15)
- for relationship with Him (Luke 8:21)
- to ensure our deeds match up to our words and grow in wisdom (Luke 6:46-49)
- as a source of blessing (Luke 11:28)
- as an illustration of the cyclical relationship between mutual love and obedience (John 15:10)
- as an evidence of our continuing friendship with Jesus (John 15:14 Amplified Version)
- as a necessary element, (and consequence), of living in God's kingdom (Matthew 7:21).

Perhaps the simplest and most easily received instruction on this matter comes from the lips of Jesus' mother at Cana; "Do whatever he tells you" (John 2:5). This is the crux of obedience. It is the essence of righteous living. It is the often neglected final element of the Great Commission of Matthew 28:19-20, namely, "...teaching them to obey everything I have commanded you". This obedience is a non-negotiable and of such import to Jesus because it is foundational to the building of His kingdom!

The difficulty with obedience to God is that it frequently seems to lead us along paths contrary to our own natural inclinations. Indeed, Paul makes nodding reference to this phenomenon in Romans 8:21-23, but nevertheless concludes on a note of triumph. Even so, for obedience, the voice of "self" has to be quietened, in order that we can hear the voice of the Spirit directing and counselling us. Then, we invariably have to step out in faith at God's prompting to our inner selves. When we are called to a measure of what may be termed radical obedience – or something greatly at odds with worldly wisdom – then elements of fear additionally need to be overcome: fear of failure, fear of ridicule, fear of incurring loss, fear of harm. All are very real obstacles to running in obedience to God's leading.

It has been our experience as a family that when God has guided us to take more radical steps, this has come with a greater clarity and surety, so that we can obey with some confidence. He is, after all, a good Dad, not a mischievous quiz-master trying to catch us out. However, whatever our guidance, and whether this calls us to radical or even mundane action, our subsequent obedience, or disobedience, demonstrates whether Jesus is, or is not, our Lord. That He *is* Lord, in an absolute sense, is without question. Our measure of obedience to His instruction and guidance reveals whether His Lordship - that we may have declared with our mouths and even believed in our hearts - is outworked through our actions, attitudes and way of life. One or two illustrations may help here.

I grew up in a Christian family and spent a good deal of my childhood and youth as part of a local church fellowship. At the age of nineteen, I fell seriously ill and was diagnosed by two doctors as having contracted polio. After a very active nineteen years filled with sports and travel, I now had to contemplate a potential future as a paraplegic. As I reflected on this, I realised that, for all of my activity and church involvement, I hadn't answered life's most fundamental concern. I knew about Jesus, in fact I knew all about Jesus, but I didn't actually know Him! Happily, I understood what I needed to do in order to remedy this and responded to the Gospel of the Cross (see Chapter 8) and asked Jesus to be my Saviour! It was then that I considered the reality of making Jesus the Lord of my life: if Jesus was to be my Lord *in fact*, and not merely in name, then I should be ready to submit to whatever He may ask. At this time a young Christian woman by the name of Joni Ericson, (now Joni Ericson Tada), was often in the Christian news. Her life and testimony were bringing much honour to God, despite her being a paraplegic through a swimming accident. The question occurred to me, "what if my life as a polio paraplegic were to bring more glory to God, rather than to recover? If Jesus really is to be Lord of my life, can I agree to this?" It took me three days of soul-searching before I could honestly say, "Yes", at which point something changed deep within in my measure of commitment to God and His purposes. And this has been borne out by the experience of my subsequent years. And the illness? It turned out to be nothing more than glandular fever, but I was never the same again: Jesus was now my Lord as well as my Saviour!

Jesus must be both Saviour and Lord of our lives. However, there are those who appear to have embraced the benefits of salvation, without similarly embracing the obligations of obedience. For some, a particular issue, or idol, occupies the place of top priority in their lives. The first priority may be "Mammon" (or money) – so that major life decisions are made according to financial considerations – however, it can equally be according to an interest, an individual, or a tribe.

When the 1994 Rwandan Genocide erupted, we were living in East Africa and staying in neighbouring Uganda. It was a very distressing time as we began to hear first-hand stories of the horror. What soon became apparent was that, in some cases, it was Christians who were rising up and killing Christians. This was clear because of the scale of the murders and the high numbers of believers in the nation as a result of the East African Revival some 40 years earlier. (This does not however diminish in any way the great acts of self-sacrificial courage by other Christians who sought to save further prospective victims from death). How could this be? These were those for whom Jesus was Saviour, but not

Lord - for whom at a time of severe trial, a different priority was exposed as ruling their actions, other than Jesus.

In similar vein, a Christian man, admitting to having participated in like fratricide explained that, "The blood of my culture is thicker than the water of my baptism"[21]. It sort of says it all!

So, Jesus is still asking His Church the same question:

> "Why do you call me 'Lord, Lord' and not do what I say?" (Luke 6:46).

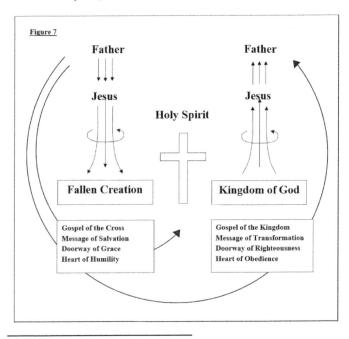

Figure 7

---

[21] Recounted by Bishop Richard Harris on the BBC Radio 4 "Today" programme.

(Appendix 1, Figure 11, shows this last diagram with the inclusion of all Biblical references).

Returning to our diagram then, (Figure 7), let us not underestimate the challenges involved in walking in obedience to the ways of God. In constructing a comparable pattern to that previously formulated for the Gospel of the Cross, (with its "Grace" and "Humility"), the doorway into the kingdom of God has already been named as "Righteousness". Now we see that the heart attitude with which we pass through this door must be a "Heart of Obedience", and these can now also be added to our illustration.

But obedience to what? To whom is beyond question if we wish to abide under the rule and reign of God in His kingdom, but to what exactly?

If we take Mary's instruction, "Do whatever he tells you" (John 2:5), at face value, then we understand that our obedience is simply to the voice of Jesus and the leading of the Holy Spirit. In practice, God speaks to us in many ways and for various purposes, but in two broadly distinctive styles. The word "Word", when we find it in our English translations, is generally a translation of one of two Greek words *rhema* and *logos*. *Rhema* indicates a specific word for a specific situation at a specific time. *Logos* refers to God's communication of His timeless truths which have relevance and importance irrespective of the occasion, country or century in which we stand.

These *rhema* words to us invariably come as personal and often powerful communications from God. They require a particular action at a particular time if we are to respond in obedience. Some of these communications may have great, life-changing significance or international impact, such as the Damascus Road encounter of Paul (Acts of the Apostles 9:1-9). Conversely, they may have less far-reaching significance but nevertheless be of crucial value to the individuals concerned.

A friend of mine was driving to work alone in her car. She was suddenly aware of a very unique toothpaste smell, common to only one brand, filling the vehicle. This was clearly so "other-worldly" as to entirely capture all of my friend's attention. She knew only one person who used this brand. Receiving this strange awareness as an instruction from God, she decided to drive as a matter of urgency to this person's house. Upon drawing up outside, she saw the front door open and the lady of the house emerging carrying two large suitcases: she was in the process of leaving her husband and children while they were absent from home. This encounter on the doorstep enabled my friend to counsel the lady and persuade her to not just "disappear", but rather to discuss her decision with the rest of her family and then proceed from there. God is interested in all of our lives. He is committed to our welfare and speaks through His *rhema* words into our situations – to be heard by those who are listening.

Our "obedience (which) leads to righteousness" (Romans 6:16, parentheses mine) requires us to follow all that God speaks to us personally in this way. No matter how radical it may appear within our own culture, we must remain mindful that delayed obedience is usually synonymous with disobedience.

What of the *logos* style material? The timeless truths which God communicates about Himself are displayed throughout the Bible. In fact, from its pages we find Jesus to be the ultimate *logos* communication from God and of God. Jesus as "the *logos*" is expressed succinctly at the start of John's gospel, where He is simply called "the Word" (John 1:1 & 14). Jesus models as 'the Word' a daily righteousness for us: we only need look to Him to see what this might look like. We also find similar instruction in Paul's letters to young churches. Here, Paul teaches on several themes, and his advice for daily righteous living can be summarised by the phrase "walking in the ways of God".

Now, walking in the "ways of God" might be best expressed by Paul's exhortation to "live by the Spirit, and you will not gratify the desires of the sinful nature" (Galatians 5:16). It is Holy Spirit's gentle leading, empowering and conviction which is our constant equipping, encouragement and correction. This is to fashion us individually into the likeness of Jesus, and corporately as the Church, into a Bride fit for His desiring. In these things we see the fulfilment of the apostle's teaching themes. So then, how do we "Live by the

Spirit"? The answer is found in the concluding verses of Galatians 5, as Paul expands on his command of verse 16.

To begin with, it is perhaps alarming that he feels the need to warn the Galatians against "...sexual immorality, impurity and debauchery, idolatry and witchcraft, hatred, discord, jealousy, fits of rage, selfish ambition, dissentions, factions and envy, drunkenness, orgies and the like...", and to sternly caution that "...those who live like this will not inherit the kingdom of God" (Galatians 5:19-21). As has already been noted, these words were written to the Galatian church, not the secular world. Similar passages are found in Ephesians 5:3-5 and in 1 Corinthians 6:9-10 – each with the warning that those who live in this way will certainly not inherit the kingdom of God. Any who thus "...sows to please his sinful nature...will reap destruction..." (Galatians 6:8a). However, anyone "...who sows to please the Spirit, from the Spirit will reap eternal life" (Galatians 6:8b). Righteousness comes not through constant effort and striving, but through 'sowing to please the Spirit', through listening to His voice and following His leading. Obedience to the voice of the indwelling Holy Spirit, cultivates His presence and transformation power so that He produces the fruit of the Spirit (Galatians 5:22-25) in our lives.

One of the wonderful and gracious things about God is that He doesn't ask us to do the impossible: only to work with Him as He achieves it in us and through us! So it is, with living in obedience to God's ways. We would normally not be able to satisfy God's standards in our daily living, however, God gives us the means to do this by His Spirit. The "fruit of the Spirit" found in Galatians 5:22-23 perfectly represents the character of Jesus.

> "But the fruit of the Spirit is love, joy, peace, patience, kindness, goodness, gentleness, faithfulness, and self-control. Against such there is no law" (Galatians 5:22-23).

This should not surprise us; after all, Holy Spirit is the "Spirit of Christ" (1 Peter 1:11), or, as noted elsewhere, the "Spirit of Jesus" (Acts of the Apostles 16:7). Holy Spirit and Jesus perfectly encompass the character of the Godhead and it is this which God seeks to grow in us. As Holy Spirit is given leave to release this character, or His fruit, through our lives, so we grow in the practise of righteousness. I write "given leave" because there is nothing automatic nor inevitable about this process. I recall being taught that "Holy Spirit is a gentleman": He never forces His will upon a person, nor shouts or bullies His way and purposes into being. Thus it is, that when He brings conviction over an aspect of our behaviour or attitude, we then need to cooperate with Holy Spirit by agreeing our need for change and repenting accordingly. As we subsequently invite Him to remake this area of our life in His image, so He is gladly able to release more of His "fruit" into, and through, our lives.

It may be worth noting here that "fruit" in Galatians 5:22 is singular. The nine character qualities displayed in verses 22 and 23 are not individual "fruits" to be picked over and selected as if on some market stall. Instead, think of an orange: one fruit, but with nine segments, or elements. All nine are available to us simultaneously from Holy Spirit. Appropriating each element into our own lives however may involve extra focus for some of them more than others.

For example, the person living under the control of a spirit of anger will require more than repentance and redirection to break through into patience and peace as their normal, settled condition. Some measure of deliverance may be involved, (which in itself does not have to be a big issue, only a necessary one), plus a subsequent remodelling of thoughts and lifestyle in this area.

This process of following His promptings and pursuing His design and purposes for us is an outworking of our obedience towards God. This is our "Living by the Spirit" as we walk in God's way.

Questions for further consideration:

a) How do you understand and define "obedience"?
b) If Jesus is truly Lord of your life, what difference has this made in your daily living and pursuits?
c) In what ways do you find God speaks His *rhema* words to you most commonly?
d) In what ways do you find God speaks to you about your behaviour?

e) How does Holy Spirit change our behaviour so as to emulate Jesus, and what successful examples of this can you provide from your own experience?

Chapter 13

"Disciple" is a Verb

Living by the Spirit may sound relatively straightforward, but the reality of putting it into operation is less simple. Our natural selves are more resistant to change than we'd like to think. So it is, that Paul uses "...teaching and correction..." so as to "...present everyone perfect in Christ" (Colossians 1:28). Perfection may initially appear a long way off, given ourselves as the raw material. A more complete understanding of Paul's "perfect" may help.

The original Greek word rendered "perfect" in Colossians 1:28 is *teleios*. This word appears 19 times in the New Testament and is translated "perfect" on ten of these occasions. On five other occasions *teleios* is translated "mature". This concept of maturity complements our understanding of "perfection": it is not something arrived at in an instant but something that is grown into, just as we grow into physical maturity. *Teleios* can also be translated "complete". Ephesians 4:13 defines maturity as "attaining to the whole measure of the fullness of Christ". The Amplified Bible translates this:

> "[That it might develop] until we all attain oneness in the faith and in the comprehension of the full and accurate knowledge of the Son of God; that [we

might arrive] at really mature manhood – the completeness of personality which is nothing less than the standard height of Christ's own perfection – the measure of the fullness of Christ, *and* the completeness found in Him" (Ephesians 4:13).

There are a variety of opinions as to what constitutes maturity. I have a relative who, at the age of sixteen, took to wandering into the living room when there was company, wearing only a vest top on his upper body and stretching his arms upwards, often next to a mirror. This somewhat unnatural behaviour puzzled me until I realised the whole exercise was intended to display his newly arrived armpit hair to all present. It was a declaration to the world at large that manhood was upon him; it was a revealing of his maturity! Spiritual maturity, or *teleios* from Ephesians 4:13, is so much more than this: it is the process in which our character is completely filled with the fullness of Jesus. Our character becomes His character.

Christian maturity has nothing to do with the length of time that we have been a Christian.

On one occasion, I wanted to drive home this point forcefully when dealing with the subject in a sermon. Just before I was due to speak, I slipped to the back of the church and, out of view, I removed my clothes, replacing them with a big white towel tied around me in the style of a baby's nappy. As the sermon was announced, I made my way from the back up the central aisle, crying like a baby, and pausing

113

here and there. One worshipper I beat softly around the head, over another I pretended to vomit, near another I pretended to flatulate – with gusto – and so on. As may be imagined, after an initial reaction of surprise and bewilderment, attitudes separated among the congregation into varying levels of amusement, disapproval, or outright offense. These last two responses, I must confess, I was happy about. Standing before the congregation I then explained that when an infant does these things it's not a problem. We expect infants to behave like this, and no harm is done. However, when a grown man in his fifties begins to hit some, vomit over others, etc., it's an altogether different matter. Serious damage can be caused to individuals, and we find it offensive. This, dear friends, is what God has to look upon every day He looks upon His Church. Men and women who have been Christians for some 20, 30, 40, 50 or more years, and yet still behaving as infants in nappies. This causes untold harm within a fellowship and damages God's reputation in the world. In grown adults, immaturity is not cute, like it might be in a new-born, instead, immaturity is an ugly thing, where the beautiful character of Jesus is painfully absent. Christian maturity has nothing to do with years spent as a Christian: it is how much our character is filled with the character of Jesus.

However, for those who advance in maturity, for those whose character is being filled with the character of Jesus, as we meet them we meet Jesus, who indwells them. His character shines through. This is Paul's *teleios* goal of "perfect" for the Colossians through teaching and correction, (Col 1:28).

Such teaching and correction is core to discipleship. Other essential and complementary elements include encouragement and the sharing of God's love, forgiveness, freedom and healing into our lives, but central to all is right teaching and correction. We see this from Jesus in the way in which He discipled His twelve followers. Repeatedly we find Jesus taking His disciples aside in the gospels to privately instruct them, or correct and rebuke them as circumstances demanded. This was both intentional and continual. It was focussed and purposeful. It was not a passive, accidental programme, but an active and strategic process.

Such is discipleship. It is not a historical concept to be observed or acknowledged, but something to be implemented throughout our lives. It involves close relationship, trust, instruction and accountability. Such a measure of intertwining and submission of lives is at best uncommon in our churches, perhaps to the extent that in most Western congregations discipleship is tragically absent. Yet at the core of the Great Commission is that we "...make disciples..." (Matthew 28:19).

Several years ago, my wife and I took a team of local church members on a mission trip to Africa. Some of the participants were testing out a possible future call into missions, and so we chose to make this three week "tasting" trip as authentic as we could in order to provide a reasonably realistic understanding. One of the team, who was a middle-aged professional, struggled with some of the usual conditions and rhythms of missionary life in community on a missions base. We gently and firmly confronted each issue with him, including moments of objection or bad attitude. He did not respond too well and his end of visit debrief was difficult as a result. However, my wife and I were able to explain that throughout this trip we had been trying to disciple him as authentically as possible in this missions situation. As this realisation sank in, his resentment evaporated and was replaced with gratitude as he reflected: "I needed this". He had never experienced such "carefronting" of his sometimes unhelpful attitudes and wilfulness. With a wry smile and a measure of profundity, he said, "You know, there are not many disciplers in the church, are there?" There are not indeed. Perhaps this has ever been the case, touched upon by Paul when he writes in 1 Corinthians 4:15, "Even though you have ten thousand guardians in Christ, you do not have many fathers..."

The simple reality is that discipleship cannot be done from the pulpit on a Sunday morning or evening. Discipleship is more than instruction; it demands interaction and an accountable relationship. Whilst some creativity may be introduced to its chosen pattern, the necessary thing is that it should be done.

Questions for further consideration:

a) How would you define Christian maturity?
b) Who do you allow, or even encourage, to correct you?
c) How do you receive correction? Easily, readily, even gladly, or with resentment?
d) Are you "perfect" already?
e) Do you want to be discipled?

Chapter 14

Practical Discipleship of People

There are a variety of models of discipleship for differing situations. These can range from one-to-one accountability pairings of disciple and discipler meeting with flexibility, to larger home groups of 15 to 20 members coming together on a regular basis. There are advantages and disadvantages to each model, but my wife and I have most benefitted from larger home groups meeting regularly. For several years, and at a very formative stage in our Christian lives, we were part of a fellowship (or discipleship) group attached to our local church. A dozen or more of us met fortnightly throughout the year. We met to increase our understanding of Jesus, to encounter Him and to become more like Him. Each session began with a time of worship during which we grew in our freedom to express to Jesus our love for Him and also to step out in the spiritual gifts such as prophecy. Prayer followed naturally, after which there followed a time of focussed teaching on a specific discipleship-related subject. This usually opened out into an opportunity to respond to God on matters over which He may have been convicting us personally through the teaching material. Often a time of personal ministry ensued. (Follow up one-to-one meetings with a group leader were also available if necessary).

Our gatherings were large enough to allow an individual to stay in the background when needed, whilst also providing a body of accountability and a reservoir of encouragement – "spurring one another on…" – throughout. We were also a ready and willing group with whom to practise ministering the spiritual gifts. This was very valuable as we were gently released into these newly acquired tools for transformation. It was in this setting that I first began to dance in praise, pray with anointing for others, discover a new depth, purpose and power to Christian living, and find a bigger missionary vision for our lives stretching into the future. It was during these fortnightly sessions that I "broke through" in previous areas of bondage, such as pride and fear, and found freedom to express a passion for Jesus without traditional reserve or embarrassment.

The church is in desperate need for local leaders - be they priests, pastors, vicars, ministers, elders, deacons or shepherds – to identify and raise up men and women from their flock who can become disciplers. Call them what you will – home group leaders, cell group leaders, connect group leaders, anything – but let their commission be to "make disciples", transforming the lives of congregation members to become more like Jesus. It is through intentional discipleship that we can release the body into a new boldness, an increased generosity, a fresh joy and depth of insight and understanding, and a greater infectious passion for Jesus. Those discipled into maturity are those who are ready to step out in radical faith and creativity, to reveal the character of Jesus and demonstrate His love for others. Isn't this what we in the Body of Christ should be longing for? Please God, let us commit to "doing" discipleship and make a start. This transformation of lives demands bold action.

There is a need to recognise and raise leaders who can not only teach these lessons, but also model them in their lives as Jesus did. These are people who are naturally disposed to demonstrate humility and vulnerability and who are prepared to love unconditionally. A Godly saint, Campbell McAlpine, once asked me how I appointed leaders. He followed his question with the advice: "look for the lovers and the feeders, and you'll not go far wrong!" With its roots clearly in John 22, it's a pretty sound rule of thumb, but remember, love confronts as well as comforts, corrects as well as celebrates, and feeding can at times be a messy business, especially with babies!

The releasing of leaders for this purpose needs to be done with care, wisdom and trust, working through relationship rather than through hierarchical disposition, status or dominance. I have found that lay leaders are best released by their pastors through an ongoing, consultative relationship. This infers a dynamic, interactive, personal and accountable process in which pastors and group leaders meet periodically for mutual sharing, input and encouragement. These are also times during which trust, support and appreciation is communicated to the lay leaders, and Biblical submission and teachability demonstrated to the pastors. Trust is essential in order that openness and transparency with each other can happen with mutual confidence. In my experience, leaders are not released by completing courses or programmes - such learning aids thinking. Instead, as leaders share their lives, they release other leaders in the Church. I learned from a wonderful Zimbabwean brother the truth, "we teach what we know, but we reproduce what we are". In this way, pastors disciple future leaders through sharing their lives, role-modelling how to lead through relationship.

Invariably, establishing such a process in a local church will take time, effort and some struggle – but it is worth it! Intentional discipleship builds the kingdom into the lives of those that love God, advancing His ultimate purpose. The raising up of disciples and leaders also builds us into the priesthood of believers we are called to be, undoing the fallacy that it is the job only of the paid pastor to disciple and build the kingdom. Also, that more and more men and women may share in this process can be a tremendous blessing to church pastors, who have a difficult job at the best of times...

There is a story told that illustrates this. Jesus, walking along the road, finds a man sitting in the gutter crying.

"What's wrong with you?" said Jesus.
"I've got a broken leg", the man replied.
"That's not a problem", said Jesus, "be healed", and the man ran off rejoicing.
A little further along the way He found another man crying in the gutter.
"What's wrong with you?" asked Jesus.

"I've got a broken heart", said the man.

"It's not a problem", replied the Master, "be healed", and the man again ran off rejoicing.

At length Jesus found yet another man sitting in the gutter crying.

"What's wrong with you?" again asked Jesus.

"I'm a pastor" said the man, and Jesus sat down in the gutter and wept also.

It's a hard, hard job being a church leader, but Jesus knows, understands and feels the pain and frustration.

In many cases, the difficulty of being a church leader is exacerbated to some extent by it being one individual who carries this responsibility for one, or sometimes several, churches. They are expected to be proficient preachers, teachers, counsellors, accountants, administrators, evangelists, public relations and publicity managers, and even experts in a number of these departments! This is clearly unrealistic, and frankly unbiblical. The pattern we find in the New Testament is what can best be termed "team leadership". Paul modelled this in his missionary endeavours and encouraged plural or team leadership groups in the churches that his ministry planted. In Ephesians 4:11 he enumerates five different leadership offices whose role is to "equip the saints", or "prepare God's people" for works of service. These are plainly separate individuals, and not intended to be one person wearing five hats. In Paul's day, we saw a pattern of *one* church in any location, but served by *many* leaders. Today we have largely turned this on its head: *many* churches in a location, but each with *one* licensed leader. Notwithstanding this, my purpose here is to highlight that any such church leader, however gifted, cannot possibly fulfil every facet of their job requirement and disciple their flock effectively. And then there's most likely this leader's family somewhere back home who would also value some time… The issue is that the way in which we "do" church in a majority of cases makes for a tough time for the man or woman in charge. If anything can be done to make the job easier, then it should be regarded as a worthwhile investment – and discipleship can!

Argentinian Christian leader, Alejandro Rodrigues, performs a tellingly hilarious sketch about the frustrations of church pastoring. God's leading and direction stand on the opposite side of a group of chairs representing "church issues" – taken to be the problems caused by immaturity among the congregation. Accompanied by his own commentary, he has to spend all his time reorganising the chairs instead of leading the people into God's bigger purposes for the church. Rearranging them, falling over them, trying to hold some apart, it's religious slapstick with a heart-breaking message. Discipleship deals with such immaturity and produces lay leaders who can help shoulder the load of pastoring.

Questions for further consideration:

a) How are you pursuing practical discipleship?

b) In what areas of your own life are you already aware of the need for change to become more like Jesus?

c) Is there someone with whom you can mutually agree to enter as a disciple into a disciple-discipler relationship?

Chapter 15

Transforming Society

As challenging as discipling individuals may, or may not, sound, transforming Christian lives has to be easier than transforming or discipling society at large. The values, culture and practises of communities can frequently be rooted in past centuries of edicts, offences, customs, prejudices and demonic preferences. Successfully bringing change to societies which are resistant to God's ideas can be a rather complex proposition. Whilst a major move of Holy Spirit over a nation has happened before, bringing conviction of wrongdoing to the masses, consideration of a more strategic approach may be a helpful place from which to start. Any campaign such as this needs to be waged in two distinct theatres: the physical and the supernatural.

On a physical level, the Church needs to release Godly men and women into the spheres of society to which they are called, namely, business, government, family, education, science, the arts and media, sports, entertainment, and so on. Their commission is demanding: to be light in dark places and to live righteous lives in unrighteous realms often in the face of ridicule, lack of comprehension and outright opposition. Just as God raised up Joseph, Daniel and Esther to positions of influence in secular systems, so He is doing the same today, for the sake of the kingdom. Those who step into these fields have at times attracted contempt or disdain from the Body for apparently falling into step with "the world system"! This cannot be. Such "ministries" which build the kingdom require from the rest of us our constant encouragement and support to sustain their effectiveness.

It may be that we are more familiar with the corruption of business or political systems or the moral decline of the media – but if we believe that God's plan for salvation is not just to pluck individuals out of this quagmire but to actually redeem society as a whole, then our great commission to go into all the world requires that Christians enter into every sphere in the name of Jesus. Jesus is raising up Godly men and women to stand in secular spaces with authority, influencing the values and operations of the realm or field in which they work. We need to view those called into these positions as our frontline evangelists and activists, building them up, not tearing them down. It is not easy work, they will be subject to the difficulties of the culture into which they enter as well as becoming prime targets for those who are enemies of God and His kingdom. If such men and women are to maintain their positions and be fruitful in rebuilding righteousness into their particular sphere of society, then the Church needs to recognise the enormity of this calling and strengthen them.

How the Church may achieve this strengthening is open to debate. Not all church leaders have experience or understanding of what life looks like in the worlds of business, entertainment, politics and so on. This can potentially cause some difficulty within discipler-disciple relationships if the church leader is discipling someone from a field of which they know little. It would be helpful for such disciplers to initially shadow those whom they disciple during a typical working week so as to increase understanding and aid future communication. An even more effective discipling relationship can result from the discipler either currently practising, or having past experience, of the disciple's working sphere of society, for example in business, as a mother, in education, politics or as a missionary. In such circumstances an immediate empathy is possible between the parties concerned. This is very helpful because the disciple feels understood, which builds confidence into the relationship.

In most of the diverse fields of society mentioned the dangers and temptations remain fairly common. In my own experience of engineering management, I have encountered bribery in an attempt to gain an advantage, been ordered to falsify evidence to enhance perceived performance, and have been set up with girls in prostitution, proffered as a perk expected to be taken by a man in my position. One might observe that our enemy lacks originality in that he only seems to sing three tunes, "Money, sex and power" (see Richard Foster's book of the same name); but they are strong and powerful tunes which can seduce most who are unaware. Yet this is our commission: to be salt and light which will restore Godly values into just such areas of our society.

> "You are the salt of the earth. But if the salt loses its saltiness, how can it be made salty again? It is no

longer good for anything, except to be thrown out and trampled by men. You are the light of the world. A city on a hill cannot be hidden. Neither do people light a lamp and put it under a bowl. Instead they put it on a stand, and it gives light to the whole house. In the same way, let your light shine before men, that they may see your good deeds and praise your Father in heaven." (Matthew 5:13-16).

We all have a position to fulfil in the "Kingdom Team", but some are providentially raised to greater visible or functional prominence. These can be thought of as the football strikers of the team, with added responsibility for scoring against the opposition and so affecting material change in the overall result. These men and women particularly need our encouragement and prayerful support as they take on the challenge of making good "the System" – of which, more later in the following chapter.

Here are some of the practical mechanics of transforming a society: changing unrighteous laws, exposing corruption, loving the unlovely, accepting the outcasts, nurturing the young, affording dignity to all, upholding justice, championing the weak, honouring sacrifice, encouraging creativity and all under the umbrella of a healthy fear of the Lord. If these are some of the mechanics, then in practical terms the objectives may be presented as:

- Politics without corruption, but rather serving the best interests of the electorate with integrity.

- Business without fraud, that creates prosperity and products to benefit the whole community.
- Family without abuse, instead providing the loving, stable nurturing environment in which to raise successive generations.
- Sport without cheating, in which fair play, skill and honest endeavour are celebrated to the enjoyment of all.
- Entertainment without sleaze, that brings pleasure and refreshment to the innocent soul.
- Science without pride, revealing and harnessing the wonders of creation for fruitful purposes.
- Education without indoctrination, investing in the development of lives for the betterment of individuals and society as a whole.
- Justice without prejudice, acting impartially to render what is right and merited to the concerned parties.
- Art without guile that celebrates the Creator's mark in each of us.
- Communication without lies in which the media presents truth balanced with wisdom to inform and instruct.
- Healthcare without profit, with care and compassion at its heart, and so on…

Can you imagine the transformation achieving such objectives would bring to any society?

Transformation cannot be achieved by mere physical activity. Our societies are invariably dominated and driven by spiritual forces (Ephesians 6:12). These must first be identified and disarmed if significant lasting change is to be achieved. As Jesus taught in Mark 3:27, the strong man has first to be bound before his home can be plundered. This is not to be approached nor attempted lightly. It is recommended that a wider campaign by many churches and Christian organisations joining together in community can be far more effective in this rather than lone congregations doing something in isolation. Unity can be a powerful tool against an adversary who delights to divide and conquer. Past initiatives such as "March for Jesus"[22] have enjoyed

---

[22] "March for Jesus" is a procession of Christian prayer and praise undertaken along public streets, predominantly in cities, to declare the Lordship of Jesus and celebrate His goodness. The first such event was organised for London in 1987 by Gerald Coates, (Pioneer Ministries), Lynn Green and Lawrence Singlehurst, (Youth With A Mission), Roger Forster, (Icthus Church Fellowship) with the musical score provided by Graham Kendrick. The self-styled vision of the "March for Jesus" movement is "To see churches unite in public worship of the Lord Jesus Christ and Christians working together to impact their city with praise, prayer and proclamation". The idea for such large scale, public events quickly spread from this initial example to other cities around the United Kingdom and also around the world. Perhaps one of the biggest of such gatherings occurred in Sao Paulo, Brazil, in 1991, attended by some three million Christians.

The format of each "March" follows a similar pattern. With musicians disposed at intervals throughout the procession, a programme of Christian songs is sung corporately in a specified order, and these are interspersed with choreographed chants, proclamations or targeted prayers. The whole event concludes with a prayer rally.

One of the consequences of this type of event is that it provides an opportunity to build unity across the Body of Christ in a location as church fellowships gather to participate from across the denominational spectrum. When Christians join together in prayer and praise, then God can use this partnership to build bridges of

significant impact in this regard. However, I would humbly suggest that ground gained by these programmes has not been securely held to date. A more targeted, strategic and sustained approach may better serve our purposes.

For the church to be effective, joined-up-church needs to be the rule instead of the exception. We are members of the same army, combatting the same enemy, in the same cause for the same King, and for one kingdom. In practice, this might look like joint prayer events with a targeted focus each time, praise breaking onto the streets, large scale community development projects, city-wide counselling and ministries to the poor and broken, or city/nation-wide orchestrated campaigns to counteract injustice, immorality, corruption or fraud in our national life. Instead of this, at times it seems that our cities are full of local churches trying to operate as though they are the only congregation in the village![23]

---

reconciliation: reconciliation across divides of theology, race, social and economic status – all of these differences becoming eclipsed by the strong hope and directed purpose we share in Christ. This is a spiritual undertaking under the leading and conviction of His Holy Spirit. Similarly, the public repentance of those engaged in the "March", articulated through the choreographed script and with heartfelt humility, has effect in the spiritual realm over the host city. Curses can be broken and blessing released as humility and unity conjoin, and this has been a common result around the world. "March for Jesus" can indeed be a powerful tool for transformation when undertaken with genuine passion, and provide a breakthrough in the heavenlies for Godly change.

[23] Here, two major aspects of Christian concern are brought together, namely, urban mission and spiritual warfare.
For some church members, the sins of the city are too great to warrant our compassion or succumb to our ministrations, however, faced with

Whilst members will be aware that around the corner is another church (albeit of a different denomination), little or no interaction will be enjoyed. Similarly, it seems that little thought is given to synergy in strategic planning for missions, community development or compassion ministries in their urban area. I have previously enjoyed membership of a number of cross-denominational ministers' meetings. However, in my experience this sense of commonality among the ministers of differing denominations rarely translates into practical joint ventures among their congregations, though they may share the same streets. Unity put into practice through the different local expressions of church is essential to the effective advancing of the kingdom.

---

the wickedness of Ninevah, God chose yet to ask, "Should I not be concerned about that great city?", (Jonah 4:11), in the face of Jonah's arguments. Furthermore, Jesus' compassion for the city that would soon cry out for His crucifixion was such that He wept over Jerusalem. Here, if nowhere else, is a clear mandate for urban mission!
In some Christian circles the matter of spiritual warfare, practically engaging the "spiritual forces of evil" in serious combat, receives scant attention. This is a great pity. Paul is very clear against whom we, the people of God, are contending in Ephesians 6:12, and in order to enjoy success in this struggle it is important to understand the spiritual authority upon which we stand, and how to effectively wield the weapons He has placed into our hands. As in any warfare, strategy is just as important as strength, although expansion on these issues is not the prime focus of this publication. Instead, some recommended titles are listed in the Bibliography herewith for further study and explanation.

For branches of local church sharing the same neighbourhood, one of the consequences arising is that they share the same prevailing social issues within their community. These may present as problems: drug addictions, poverty, crime, prostitution, unemployment, and the like, or as resources: prosperity, high standard of education, good healthcare, strong sense of community, etc. Whilst different congregations may feel led to target different issues within their common pond, there can be no escaping the fact they nevertheless are all in the same boat, sharing a common local mission-field.

The idea of what comprises a "mission-field" has traditionally been confined to some foreign land in which dwell "the heathen"; this picture being particularly reinforced by the Christian missionary societies of Europe and America from the 18th Century onwards. In more recent times, with the global population enjoying much greater mobility – whether by choice or through force of circumstance – we have seen large numbers of people never having heard of Jesus arrive upon our shores and settle in our own local neighbourhoods. This has given rise to the very legitimate realisation that we can be missionaries to "the nations" without even having to leave our native country. Typical examples within the United Kingdom would include the Somalis of Cardiff, Pakistanis of Bradford and the Chinese of Manchester. The world has come to us instead of our necessarily needing to "go" to the world. Even so, a sense has remained amongst the many that missionary activity is most properly directed to "other nationals" as opposed to indigenous Britons. How wrong this is!

As Paul writes in Romans 3:23, "...*all* have sinned and fallen short of the glory of God", so *all* are needful of the hope, help and healing that the gospel brings, and of the life transforming message of God's kingdom. The question with which we, the *ekklesia*, have to wrestle, is what strategies should we employ to best achieve God's intended purposes: how will He lead us? Strategic missions is a vast and comprehensive consideration of study and practice, and one helpful device seeks to identify trends or similarities within population groups so as to aid the formulation of more focussed, or targeted, missions programmes in each area. Such groupings may have nothing whatever to do with ethnicity, but rather be identified by profession, (e.g. financial services personnel, or girls in prostitution), personal circumstance, (e.g. young mothers, or those who are drug dependant), location, (e.g. a housing estate), or any other perceived common denominator within a given community. These become target groups, for which appropriate strategies may be sought from God to reach into these sub-groups of the population with relationship and the love of Jesus. It's a good, God-given strategy – after all, Jesus was Himself known for associating with some of His society's groupings. (and some of the less respectable ones at that!), – but such a focussed, targeted approach can be costly...

134

Some years ago I had the honour of working alongside a local congregation in Nottingham, UK, and a team of ladies focussed upon reaching out to the many girls around their neighbourhood working in prostitution. These ladies would be out on the streets with the girls night after night, offering hot drinks and a caring, listening ear. As relationships and trust grew, these Christian women would attend court hearings with the girls to provide some moral support, help with childcare, education and untold other aspects as the girls themselves battled debt, addictions or violent exploitation by those "controlling" them. The costs came physically to these ladies in being out on the streets through the night several times a week, and emotionally in the disappointments of sometimes seeing trust broken or hopes shattered. Nevertheless, they *did* see lives changed, healed and made whole!

A different type of price can be demanded of those adopting an incarnational approach to targeting a particular missions focus group. A man I knew in Youth With A Mission, (Germany), felt called to the punk and "Goth" communities in the city where he lived. After months of fruitlessly trying to engage with them, this "respectable" young husband and father took a significant decision. He visited a barber who shaved his head, but for a spiked, black "Mohawk" crest, bought a new set of black clothes and underwent several body piercings, including on his face – and then had a shock. When he walked into his bank, where he was previously known and welcomed, he was greeted only with suspicion and coldness, similarly so on public transport where people avoided sitting next to him. He was surprised to discover the intense feelings of rejection that he was constantly meeting, and realised that this was the normal daily experience of his missions target group. It caused him to change his approach completely to how he reached out to the punks and Goths of his city – by whom he was now accepted – but now with some marked success.

The point I wish to make here is that if we are to transform our society, and, by implication, all of its constituent parts, then we will need to rethink our traditional missionary programmes and means of working. Wherever we are, we live in the middle of mission fields, and a strategically targeted approach to groups within these has been proven to be effective.

Questions for further consideration:

a) Why is God interested in society?
b) What Biblical evidence is there to suggest that our secular and spiritual worlds are mutually exclusive?
c) Does a "mission target group" have to be defined solely by ethnicity or location? By what other criteria could they be identified?
d) To what sphere of society have you been called and equipped for the purpose of transformation?
e) How are you approaching this commission, i) spiritually, and ii) physically?

Chapter 16

Transforming "The System"

In our previous chapter we have noted some specific initiatives upon which joined-up churches could immediately embark in order to put kingdom principles into practice, (such as accepting the outcasts, city-wide community development projects, nurturing the young, etc.), however, other aspects of societal transformation, (such as changing unrighteous laws, addressing the evils of systemic poverty), require "the System" to receive some serious modification. A common complaint, heard in nations around the world and especially at election times, is that "You may change the party or government in power, but you can't change the System!" There is perhaps a deal of truth in this, largely because whilst governments can be voted out in a fairly-run democratic election, spiritual powers ruling over societies and nations cannot, and there is an unmistakeable spiritual dimension to "the System".

In referring to "the System" I mean to draw attention to an essence which permeates the undertakings of societies, be this at city, national or international levels. This "essence" is such that even well-intentioned leaders find that their efforts to improve their sphere of responsibility are frequently frustrated, as though an invisible corrupting agent is at work within their organisation. This is pretty near the mark, these "corrupting agents" being supernatural in nature, and intent on pursuing their demonically driven agenda. Floyd McClung comments on this in particular relation to cities in his book "Spirits of the City"[24], and a few examples are shown below;

> "Corporate sin in the life of a city also gives Satan a foothold over the city and institutions within it"

> "Where Biblical unity exists, we can... get on with the business of challenging the powers[25] and their influence in public institutions and policy."

> "Like a battlefield after a war, the cities of our world often look like war zones. There is physical destruction and spiritual despair. Decades of welfare programmes have not turned the tide, nor has the recent bent towards conservative economic policies. Because cities have a spiritual dimension, they will only be changed by those who perceive the spiritual nature of the battle for our cities and exercise true spiritual authority."

Whilst a detailed treatment of these spiritual strongholds may be found elsewhere, (see the appended Bibliography), I want here to address some of the key practical areas which must be targeted in the physical to complement the campaign of spiritual warfare being simultaneously waged in the heavenlies. Both dimensions of spiritual and physical are equally important. Both also require champions who will

---

[24] "Spirits of the City" by Floyd McClung, published by Kingsway.
[25] The context of this word "powers" is of demonic personages.

lead, direct and spearhead kingdom advances, and some practical theatres for these advances are now suggested below. However, I believe it to be critical for success that underpinning these "champions'" activities is a body of support, a "Movement" if you will, calling for a like-minded transformation in the socio-cultural life of a country. There is an opinion that for change to be sustained within a nation, then three spheres of society have to be brought into conjunction: the political, the economic and the socio-cultural.[26] Estimates vary as to what percentage of the population needs to comprise this Movement, but some consider less than 10% to be sufficient. If this is correct, then surely this could be within the scope of church memberships in many nations – if only they would commit together to this vision.

Now in so far as some strategic theatres of engagement are concerned with a view to affecting "the System", the following areas of importance immediately present themselves. Politics, Economics and Commerce, Education, the Media and, mindful of its long-term potential to influence government opinion, Environmental concerns.

The Political System

Regarding the United Kingdom, one area of interest has to be that of political corruption and fraud. This is nothing new.

---

[26] A paper by Nicamor Perlas providing further explanation, (in this case concerning the Philippines), can be found at www.globenet3.org/Essays/Essay_Change.shtml : "What Would it Take to Change a Nation State?"

For centuries the seat of government has been a place where material advantage can be bought. Members of Parliament have accepted bribes to ask leading questions in The House, others have been in the pay of commercial concerns, charged with safeguarding their company's interests, whilst others have been sponsored, (funded), by organisations having very clear agendas of their own. All of this, irrespective of their constituents' good.[27] Heads of government have been no less reticent to cross boundaries of integrity to force through their political programmes. In the "stick" mode of a "carrot and stick" approach, extreme pressure has been exerted by governments upon their MPs to force through legislation regarding which some Members have been averse on grounds of conscience. At the opposite end of the spectrum of persuasion, honours, including knighthoods, have been promised as rewards for compliance to politicians unwilling to toe the party line. The result has been an erosion of trust and respect for our elected representatives, and for the democratic system of government by which we are ruled.

Political scandals have been persistently reported by the media which have caused an outcry among the electorate. These perhaps culminated in the furore over the flagrant misuse of some Members of Parliaments' expense allowances in 2009, and this at a time of severe recession and hardship among the public at large. Consequently, the

---

[27] A much more detailed treatment of the ills of British politics may be found in "The Truth About Westminster" by Patrick Dixon and published by Kingsway.

principle is now well established in the UK that politicians' financial dealings should be open for scrutiny by all. Here is a gifted opportunity for Christians to be vocal in requiring righteousness to be the normal standard of behaviour for our political representatives. We need to see truth, integrity, dignity and righteousness in our system of government. In fact, we need to see Christians in government!

On a wider note, it is very clear that political corruption and fraud are not limited to the British Houses of Parliament...

The Economic System

Another building block of "the System" within a nation concerns the economy. Economic theory, what constitutes good and what constitutes bad practice, and, importantly, in whose interests, has ever been a realm of heated debate. Among other considerations, disputes variously revolve around the measure of government intervention to maintain a buoyant economy, versus the release of all imposed controls so as to rely solely upon free market forces to drive an economy at national level. For a given country, these concerns are clearly a matter for domestic governmental choice. Notwithstanding this, there is a rather more sinister economic game played out on the international stage whereby, (generally speaking), richer nations dictate to poorer nations what system they are to adopt, and what legislative changes must be made in the poorer nations' laws and procedures. This external manipulation of the domestic affairs of sovereign states is principally achieved through what Ha-Jong Chang calls the "Unholy Trinity" of the

International Monetary Fund, (IMF), the World Bank, and the World Trade Organisation, (WTO).[28] These three institutions are largely controlled by the rich countries, with the IMF and World Bank being part of the United Nations system. Unfortunately, and in an admittedly sweeping simplification, through these organs the poorer nations of the world are denied the means of prosperity from which the richer nations became rich. This is the maintenance of systemic poverty on a global scale, and constitutes a flagrant injustice. Clearly, enormous change is required here at international level if God's kingdom values are to predominate in the world's economic system.

Such change will not happen without being driven forward by those seeking to bring a righteous transformation to these practices biased towards the rich. At one time the established church could have been looked to as a powerful agent to achieve such change, but things are not the way they were… The role of the church in influencing governments and international relations – illustrated well by the influence of the church in medieval Europe – has significantly diminished in recent generations. Instead, this influence has been gladly assumed by the business community. It is to business that governments now look to deliver or sustain prosperity, and with no small measure of self-interest. In the circumstances, we need the Christian business communities

---

[28] This, from "Bad Samaritans. The Guilty Secrets of Rich Nations and the Threat to Global Prosperity". Ha-Jong Chang, published by Random House Books.

to find their voice in these matters. In rich nations, to call for a fairer means by which the business of all nations can be transacted, and in those poorer nations which fall prey to this system, to join as one in refusing to play this game anymore and stepping out in the development of homegrown manufacturing industries, adding value in-country to their natural resources prior to marketing their wares elsewhere. These are issues of international justice in which the Church, God's *ekklesia,* must concern herself.

The Education System

Now, what about education? In May 2001, British Prime Minister Tony Blair said,

> "Our top priority was, is and always will be education, education, education. At a good school, children will gain the basic tools for life and work. But they ought also to learn the joy of life…And they learn the value of life: what it is to be responsible citizens who give something back to their community."[29]

This is vastly different to the historical view that education is all about becoming proficient in the "3 R's". In fact, it has much more to do with an holistic idea of education, incorporating socio-cultural, religious and moral elements as well as the traditional academic content of the syllabus. Even

---

[29] Speech by the Rt. Honourable Tony Blair, UK Prime Minister, launching the Labour Party education political manifesto on 23rd May 2001.

more so, I believe, this model is closely akin to a style of education appropriate to kingdom of God values, where material is formulated and delivered from a Biblical worldview. Here, the whole person of the student is addressed, and scope is additionally provided to recognise and equip leavers with vocational abilities, to grow in life skills and to mature in character development.

Impossible? Not really. Such a programme of learning has been pioneered by Youth With A Mission, an organisation committed among other things to training and education worldwide. The College of Education of this organisation's University of the Nations has produced just such a syllabus, and this is being delivered with notable success in many countries. Some years ago I visited such a school in Tema, Ghana, which ranged from nursery classes to pre-university age, with a learning complement of 500 pupils or more. There was a waiting list of children of all ages for enrolment, and among the student body there numbered eleven from the families of Members of Ghana's Parliament, and numerous sons and daughters of lawyers, doctors and other professional classes. This was no weak attempt at "doing something Christian in a small corner": it was, and remains, a successful, God-centred learning establishment of repute.

If the traditional scheme of education is to be thus expanded and presented from a Biblical worldview, consideration must be given to those charged with delivering this programme. A maxim already noted says that, "We teach what we know, but we reproduce what we are". It is indeed true, as pupils are more likely to imitate what is modelled to them rather than what is instructed at them, and this then brings the behaviour of teachers into focus. From time to time debate circles around the suitability of persons with high ability but low morality to be entrusted with public office. (Not least among such are our political leaders!). In many societies "Doing" and "Being" are considered to be mutually exclusive aspects of an individual, but this surely cannot be so for this new breed of educators. Godliness and moral rectitude are caught and not taught: these are high standards indeed, but we would not expect that which is accepted and normal in the dominion of darkness to be inspiring kingdom of God values, would we? We need to see Godly men and women raised up in the teaching profession who can influence "the System" of education as well as the next generation!

The Media

It is popularly acknowledged that truth is a casualty of war. However, it seems to be similarly afflicted these days by peace. A 2021 survey found that only 44% of Britons now trust the British Broadcasting Corporation, (BBC), to report the truth. It would appear that scepticism knows no bounds, falling upon this once august and revered institution as well as the British tabloids and broadsheets alike. Let's face it, mistrust of our media industry is not without considerable provocation. The erstwhile art of propaganda, and the barefaced vice of lying have now graduated to more palatable titles as "misinformation", being "economical with the truth" and now "fake news". It could be argued that this erosion of certainty has been accelerated by Postmodernism where "my truth" does not have to agree with "your truth", even when concerning the same fact. Whatever the case, it is clear that those vested interests controlling and directing our media news outlets have become comfortable with presenting "their truth" in ways that serve their purposes – be these political, commercial or cultural.

With regards to standards in our entertainment media, the industry is similarly conformed "to the pattern of this world"[30] rather than to that of the kingdom. Certainly, in Western nations, the entertainment industry plays an enormous part in the lives of citizens. Our fashions, tastes, opinions, values and dreams are vastly influenced by television programmes and social media outlets, which we consume for hours every day in the intimacy of our homes. It is difficult to judge just what is discipling what: society the entertainment media, or the other way around as seemingly almost every year we see another boundary crossed which would have been condemned a decade or so earlier. Broadcasting standards are specified by governments the world over, and those responsible for formulating and maintaining these standards hold tremendous responsibility – and power.

In 1963 a British woman, Mary Whitehouse, launched a movement in the United Kingdom known as the National

---

[30] Romans 12:2

Festival of Light. It was intended to arrest the slide to what was then termed the "permissive society", and particularly targeted the increasing measures of sex and violence on our TV screens. Her campaign, frequently interacting with Central Government, was sustained for decades, but ultimately failed to affect any material change. Springing out of her devoutly Christian values, her views were, however, judged by many to be "Edwardian", some 60 or more years out of date, and she met with persistent public ridicule despite achieving some notable successes in other spheres of her campaigning. Whatever our opinions as to how genuine were Mary's concerns in her day, her story nevertheless illustrates what opposition is to be encountered by any who attempt to reverse the unrighteous trend in these media standards towards kingdom values. It's a hard road to walk, and promises to be a painful one at that, the reason being simple – as has been written before: sex sells – as does violence! God raise up men and women whose commitment to truth, beauty and righteousness in our media concerns will be sufficient to withstand the withering opposition of the world systems.

The Environment

Another area of concern ripe for vocal Christian intervention is the protection of our world environment against exploitation and outright destruction. As we progress through the third, fourth and fifth decades of this 21st Century I see the state of our environment becoming more and more *the* consuming issue on the international stage as

"Doomsday" indications are allegedly triggered, and blame bounced between nation states. A recently heard Christian "do nothing" defence of "it's all going to get renewed by God when He makes a new heaven and a new Earth anyway" is just not acceptable! We have a clear mandate and responsibility to steward and preserve that which God made "very good", (Genesis 1:31). There are some passionate organisations and pressure groups championing the cause of environmental responsibility, and besides the increasing vocalism of Extinction Rebellion, perhaps Greenpeace enjoys a pre-eminence of enduring longevity among these. However, where is the strong voice of the established church in all of this throughout the past decades? Pope Francis and Justin Welby, Archbishop of Canterbury, have both been vociferous on the world stage of environmental concern, but this is seldom being mirrored at local level. Thank God that there are Christian men and women who are environmental activists, but shouldn't the global church be no less assertive? Governments are good at making well-meaning promises for change when placed under an international spotlight at large multi-national summits, but less adept at delivering on their environmental promises. Who can hold a government to account and, on a broader stage, who can teach a nation righteousness? Here, surely, lies the role of the Church.

It seems to me that in all of these matters we are crying out for God to raise up a deep people from within His Church who, as mothers and fathers can disciple not only the many, but also the nations. For this indeed is the process necessary to realign current world "Systems" with the righteousness and justice for which God Himself cries out through His Old Testament prophets. These will be the people who, without any doubt, know exactly what on Earth they are doing; who understand the mission of God to advance His kingdom, who recognise and accept their part in these purposes, and who know God's message of redemption is not just for their personal eternity, but is for the "now" of society also.

Many of these people will not see themselves as "ministers" in the conventional sense of that word; they will be politicians, business people, artists and performers, educators, activists and campaigners, journalists, engineers, medical professionals and voices on the streets and in the communities where God has been pleased to plant them so that they may bear His fruit in due season. These are those whom Ed Silvoso terms "marketplace ministers"[31], and who have a key role in transforming society, transforming "the System" and building the kingdom.

If we remain content to keep the spiritual and the secular aspects of life at arms' length, jogging along, as it were, in two simultaneous but parallel universes which never meet, then we have failed. Failed as God's *ekklesia*, ignoring the commission which this Jesus-given title embodies to *lead*

---

[31] See "Transformation" Chapter 6, "Bridging the Pulpit and the Marketplace" by Ed SIlvoso, published by Chosen Books.

and provide *governance* over the nations – discipling them and teaching them to obey all that God has commanded.[32]

Questions for further consideration:

a) How aware have you been that there is a spiritual dimension to the workings of society?
b) Have you ever tried to change "the System" in any particular field? What happened?
c) To which sphere of the marketplace do you feel called and equipped to "minister"?
d) How do you integrate the spiritual and secular dimensions of life in your daily living?

---

[32] This, drawn from the Great Commission; Matt 28:19,20.

Chapter 17

Conclusion: "Can We Built It? Yes, We Can!"

This, then, is a call to the intentional building of God's kingdom - building the kingdom not only within each person but in every sphere of society, through the strategic engagement of the Church[33]in every facet of life.

For many church members this may come as a challenge: a challenge to review their past effectiveness in transforming their own lives and their neighbourhoods; a challenge to assess how present activities impact their communities and a challenge to reshape, or affirm, their future vision for ministry as God's people. Such a process will necessarily demand a good deal of honesty, as well as humility. It is likely to be uncomfortable. However, such a review can be facilitated by asking of each plan, programme or activity, "is this of God?" and proceeding accordingly.

Considering how to intentionally build the kingdom may require the practice and focus of different expressions of church to make differing adjustments. Models of church vary, influenced by tradition, location, theology, the preferences of leaders and congregations, and the demands of the neighbourhoods in which they sit. Models at the extreme ends of the spectrum could be characterised by,

---

[33] A reminder that "Church" refers to the born-again community, Jesus' *ekklesia* of Matthew 16:18, irrespective of denomination or domicile.

1) a circle of believers, whose focus is inwards and upwards, and

2) a circle of believers whose focus is outwards.

These are illustrated in Figures 8 and 9.

Figure 8

The first example represents a very "spiritual" church. People from such a community delight in enjoying the presence of the Lord in their midst, responding with extravagant praise and worship. They revel in bathing in the richness and excitement of His being with them and upon them as they gather together. It is as though they are experiencing a foretaste of heaven itself whilst still here on earth. For such a community, diluting this with other concerns is tantamount to sacrilege, and time spent other than in worship is time wasted. The difficulty with such a community is that they can be so tightly knit, intense and other-worldly in their engagement with the Almighty that there is seldom room for others from "outside" breaking into their circle. With their focus only ever "upward", as a church they have little impact upon society at large. Whilst they co-exist with society, they do this in almost mutually exclusive worlds.

The second example is pretty much at the opposite end of the spectrum. It represents a "social" church which delights in demonstrating compassion and bringing the hurting and hopeless within its circle. This circle "rescues the perishing", but to what exactly? The lack of "upward connection" renders them powerless to affect real spiritual transformation in lives littered with spiritual wreckage.

Figure 9

A fitting reorientation for both would be for each member to face the back of their neighbour in a circumferential arrangement, and have their inner arm raised to God with their other reaching out to man. I would suggest this model to be more consistent with practical kingdom building. It provides a living demonstration of the truth of Emmanuel - "God with us" – releasing the resources of heaven to impact upon the affairs of humanity. A final illustration depicts this model of church (Figure 10).

Figure 10

God has revealed His longing to see the world and all that is in it restored rightfully under His sovereign authority. He further desires the virtues found in His character to be manifest in human lives and society at large, and the way we

154

have been "doing church" thus far is just not proving to be sufficiently effective. He is seeking the fulfilment of the prayer, "your kingdom come… on earth as it is in heaven" (Matthew 6:10), which has been given to the Church to be a heart cry. God wants His kingdom back, and the outworking of lives surrendered to Jesus needs to serve this purpose.

Some paradigm shifts are called for. Traditionally we have nurtured the image of the missionary as one who lives in a far-flung, isolated spot, enduring a lonely existence due to the nature of their vocation, giving themselves in equal measure to piety and poverty in the hope that "someday" their sacrifice of self may bear some fruit. However, men and women called to reach out to the poor or marginalised in their home nation must be also understood as radical missionaries.

I spent ten years working in urban mission in England. I can testify that doing this can be harder than working on a distant continent, which I have also done. Congregations can question why they should financially support such a worker for just "living at home". It is time to accept that a missionary is one who is both called and sent by God into a specific field to bring light, righteousness and good news from God into that field. This is a significant step towards understanding where I believe God wants to lead us.

Thus, contemporary missionaries are not only those sent to the poor or marginalised, (whether in their own nation or another), but to any sphere of influence in society in which they can intentionally advance the kingdom. This would include politics, healthcare, education and so on. If we can stretch our thinking to seeing the world of business, for example, as a field into which God wants to bring His light, His righteousness and good news, then we need to assume He is calling appropriately equipped men and women into this work also – as an expression of missions. Access to this field reasonably demands that these "missionaries" are immersed in the business world, maybe as a manager, a CEO or a chartered professional, most likely continuing to draw salaries, but no less "sent ones" than the overseas doctor or pastor. These are God's typical "marketplace ministers". It's time to recognise that God is calling a kaleidoscope of people, professions and persuasions into outward facing missions *exactly where they are*. These are those with a heart to transform their street, their workplace, their school, their friendship circles and values. They are those who recognise "the (world) System" to have its roots in the supernatural soil of God's enemies, and feel constrained to win this ground back to the kingdom. Their goal is to see love, joy, peace, patience, kindness, justice, truth, unity, forgiveness – in fact, the character of God – become normal expressions of daily life in the world around them. This is the outworking of building His kingdom here. Can this be achieved? Yes, it can! Can *we* build this? Yes, we can! But...

This requires that our church organisations encourage, strengthen, support and commission such individuals to take up these roles with a sense of vocation. It also requires that church communities facilitate these "sent ones" to network across fellowships, cities, denominations and countries, in the same way as if they had taken a Bible and mosquito net prior to boarding a plane and waving their family goodbye. We need to change our mindset around missions. It is time to envision the ordinary 9am-5pm working women and men of our local communities as a 'homeland battalion' missionary force, transforming our own society from the inside. These "sent ones" must be commissioned and released by the Church into our societies as genuine, vital expressions of *ekklesia*, who are actively getting on with the job at the sharp end of bringing transformation. Simultaneously, we, the Church, need to recognise, release and support Christian voices speaking out on the world stage addressing the international evils of injustice, corruption, immorality, systemic poverty, greed, aggression, prejudice, and "the System(s)" which beget and then maintain such wickedness. Please God, raise up "forceful men and women" (Matthew 11:12) who are more afraid of living without purpose than they are of dying for one! And then let them be released into the fields of your choosing.

All of the foregoing, no matter how big the challenge, is not an impossible dream. Indeed, it is no less than our God Almighty who wishes to accomplish the building of this kingdom through His people. So, can we build it? Yes, we can!

If we can withstand the external pressures to conform to this world, and be ourselves transformed, then we may yet go on to prove and, please God, to demonstrate His good and perfect will: to "Build the Kingdom".[34]

Lord, let it be!

Questions for further consideration

a) How is your local church reaching "upwards" and "outwards"?
b) What can you do to broaden the vision of your Christian community to include the transformation of society?
c) Will you accept God's commission to "Build the Kingdom"?

---

[34] From Romans 12:2.

Appendix I

Figure 11: Diagram with all the Bible references.

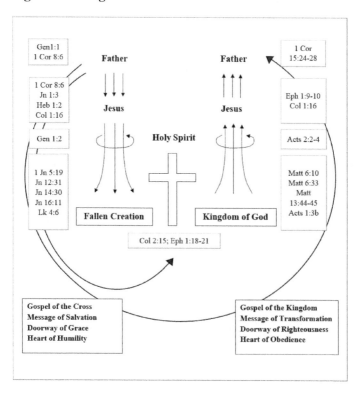

Bibliography

George Kinoti, *Hope For Africa And What The Christian Can Do,* (International Bible Society, 1997).

N.T. Wright, *How God Became King,* (SPCK, 2012).

Richard Foster, *Money, Sex And Power*, (Hodder and Stoughton, 2009).

Floyd McClung Jnr and Kalafi Moala, *Nine Worlds To Win,* (Youth With a Mission, 1998).

John Sentamu (editor), *On Rock Or Sand*, (SPCK, 2015).

Patrick Dixon, *Out Of The Ghetto And Into The City*, (Paternoster Press, 1995).

Myles Monroe, *Rediscovering The Kingdom*, (Destiny Image, 2010).

John Dawson, *Taking Our Cities For God*, (Charisma House, 2002).

Stephen Tomkins, *The Clapham Sect*, (Lion Hudson, 2010).

Floyd McClung, *Spirits Of The City*, (Kingsway, 1990).

Peter Adams, *Preparing For Battle,* (Kingsway, 1987).

Gregory Boyd, *God At War*, (Inter-Varsity Press, 1997).

Dean Sherman, *Spiritual Warfare For Every Christian*, (Youth With A Mission, 1992).

C. Peter Wagner, *Breaking Spiritual Strongholds In Your City*, (Monarch Books, 1993).

Patrick Dixon, *The Truth About Westminster*, (Kingsway, 1996).

Ha-Jong Chang, *Bad Samaritans. The Guilty Secrets Of Rich Nations And The Threat To Global Prosperity*, (Random House Books, 2007).

Ed Silvoso, *Transformation. Change The Marketplace And You Change The World*, (Chosen Books, 2007).

Ed Silvoso, *Anointed For Business*, (Chosen Books, 2002).

Ed Silvoso, *Ekklesia*, (Chosen Books, 2014).

Tim Davidson, *Passport. A Believer's Guide To The Kingdom Of God*, (Vineyard International Publishing, 2006).

Winkie Pratney, *Youth Aflame 2.0. A Manual For Discipleship*, (Independently published, 2017).

Acknowledgements

Without doubt I am extremely grateful to my wife and family who, amongst many more things, have shared since the 1980's in a missionary call to Africa and within the United Kingdom.

My gratitude also is to Keith Miller, now with Jesus, without whose challenge, support and encouragement this book would not have been written.

Moreover, there is a host of individuals who have contributed to my own growth, understanding and development as a believer, some appearing in the pages of this book although not identified by name, including Ian and Dorothy White, Oliver Nyumbu, Laurence Singlehurst, Peter Parkin, Ken McGreavy, Rostand Mana Shemahamba, Tony Hodges, David McNeil and Richard Mayers.

Finally, I wish to thank Matthew Eason for the design of the front cover, Patrick Johnstone for his helpful advice and direction, James Crockford for his theological input, Stephen Liondo for his New Testament Greek, James Bewsey for his support with desktop publishing and Beverley Samways for her wise advice, suggestions and editorial skill in bringing this work to publication.

Ed Ravenhall is married with two daughters, also married, and five grandchildren, all living in the Scottish Borders of the United Kingdom. Previously a chartered engineer, he and wife Sue have worked on staff with Youth With A Mission in both Africa and Britain for over 30 years, and this continues. In this capacity he provides teaching to diverse groups at home and abroad, undertakes community development projects in Africa and mentors Christian leaders. He has a passion to see the kingdom of God birthed in reality, not only in people's personal lives, but also in the values of society at large, so transforming nations.

Edward N. Ravenhall

ravenhalls@hotmail.com

Printed in Great Britain
by Amazon

65249962R00098